Who tore a lion apart with his bare hands? *(See page 19)*

What is the first color mentioned in the Bible? *(See page 159)*

Who amazed his shipmates by surviving the bite of a viper? *(See page 13)*

What wealthy man had fourteen thousand sheep? *(See page 21)*

What tree was a symbol of elegance? *(See page 43)*

What did the author of Proverbs admire the snake for? *(See page 17)*

Who is the first child mentioned in the Bible? *(See page 89)*

What king suffered from a crippling foot disease? *(See page 135)*

Who gave his hot-tempered brother twenty donkeys as a goodwill gesture? *(See page 37)*

What four creatures did God send as plagues on the Egyptians? *(See page 13)*

Who put a curse on an unproductive fig tree? *(See page 47)*

What ninety-year-old woman had a baby? *(See page 103)*

What color do the armies of heaven wear? *(See page 163)*

. . . and more than 1,500 other challenging questions about nature and home life in the Bible . . .

P9-DTF-081

The Best of
Bible Trivia

◇ 2 ◇

PALACES
POISONS
FEASTS &
BEASTS

J. STEPHEN LANG

LIVING BOOKS®
Tyndale House Publishers, Inc.
Wheaton, Illinois

1. Castle photo: Ruth M. Schroeppel
2. Peacock photo: Animals Animals
copyright © 1980 Zig Leszczynski
3. Front cover cartoons: copyright ©1990
Ron Wheeler

*The Best of Bible Trivia 2: Palaces, Poisons,
Feasts, and Beasts* is selections from *The
Complete Book of Bible Trivia,* copyright © 1988
by J. Stephen Lang, published by Tyndale House
Publishers, Inc.

Scripture quotations, unless otherwise noted, are
from the King James Version of the Bible.

Living Books is a registered trademark of Tyndale
House Publishers, Inc.

Library of Congress Catalog Card Number 89-51308
ISBN 0-8423-0465-7
Copyright © 1988 by J. Stephen Lang
All rights reserved
Printed in the United States of America

96 95 94 93 92 91 90
9 8 7 6 5 4 3 2

To Mark Fackler,
who is a friend of the Bible
and who understands laughter

Contents

Preface

Can we speak of *the Bible* and *trivia* in the same breath? Can this inspired document that is read with great seriousness by pastors, scholars, and lay people provide material for leisure—or even laughter?

It can. As I began writing these trivia books, I became convinced that the Bible, the divine book through which God's Truth shines, is also an earthy collection of people and incidents that can amuse (as well as enlighten) any reader. I believe that the Bible has come down to us through God's initiative. I also believe that God chose to present his truth through stories, oracles, and letters that not only inspire us, but also captivate us as all good stories do. People have recognized for centuries that the Bible is a treasure trove of stories, as attested to by the many poems, plays, novels, films, paintings, and sculptures that are based on the Scriptures.

The Bible is full of sublime teaching—and sometimes pathetic, sometimes amusing pictures of the world. It evokes tears and laughter, repulsion and admiration. To probe its many stories cannot be wrong. To ask questions about its content can, at the very least, provide innocent amusement. Even better, asking questions can lead us deeper into the content and make us appreciate and (it is hoped) study more deeply this fascinating treasury of stories.

This is not the first collection of questions and answers about the Bible, and it probably will not be the last. However, most previous books focused on the seriousness of the text, neglecting the possibilities of finding things to chuckle over and cry over. Too many of these volumes have been painfully dry.

I have avoided dryness at all costs. The arrangement here is topical, with such diverse topics as "Snakes and Other Creepy Things," "Under the Influence," "Multiple Marriages," and so on—all topics having to do with nature and domestic life. I hope the choice of topics will itself provide some chuckles. And the category "Not to Be Taken Seriously" is just for laughs. One can't include *every* subject, of course, but the range is wide—birds, animals, plants, food and drink, homes, marriages, children, burials, and many others. And while this volume of *The Best of Bible Trivia* focuses on everyday life in the Bible, Volumes 1 and 3 cover many other subjects. In all, there are more than 1,500 questions arranged under more than 50 topical headings in this book.

This book is meant for browsing. It was made to fill up your time commuting on the train, waiting at the dentist's office, before dinner is on the table, on the freeway when you and the other two people in the back seat are in the mood for a game of "quiz me." In other words, the book is designed to be read randomly, anywhere, and with no preparation of any kind. It is designed to entertain the person who unashamedly likes to be entertained—and challenged.

The author would like to hear from any person who is able to correctly (and without peeking at the answers on the back of each page) answer every question in this book. In doing the research for this book, the author himself learned quite a bit, but not enough to answer every question correctly—at least, not yet.

Happy reading! I hope you enjoy getting better acquainted with the divine—and very human—Book of books.

PART 1
Beasts and Birds and Such

✦Some Amazing Animals

1. What four creatures did God send as plagues upon the Egyptians?
2. What venomous creature bit Paul on the hand but did not harm him?
3. What did Jesus use to feed the five thousand?
4. Where did Jesus send the legion of unclean spirits he had cast out of a man?
5. What did Peter find with a coin in its mouth?
6. What did God send to destroy the vine that shaded the sulking prophet Jonah?
7. When children laughed at Elisha for his baldness, what appeared that mauled the children?
8. What croaking birds fed Elijah in his solitude by the brook Cherith?
9. What two animals owned by the Philistines carried the ark of the covenant back to Israel?
10. What foreign prophet had a talking donkey to ride on?
11. What bird served as food for the Israelites in the wilderness?
12. What animals, considered rather loathsome in Bible times, ate the carcass of Jezebel?
13. What did God provide as a sacrifice in substitute for Isaac?
14. What miraculous animals parted Elijah and Elisha as Elijah was taken by a whirlwind into heaven?

✦Some Amazing Animals (Answers)

1. Frogs, lice, flies, and locusts (Exodus 8, 10)
2. A viper (Acts 28:3-6)
3. Two fish and five barley loaves (John 6:9-12)
4. Into a herd of swine (Mark 5:13)
5. A fish (Matthew 17:27)
6. A worm (Jonah 4:7)
7. Two she-bears (2 Kings 2:24)
8. Ravens (1 Kings 2:11)
9. Two cows (1 Samuel 6:7-12)
10. Balaam of Moab (Numbers 22:28)
11. Quail (Exodus 16:13)
12. Dogs (2 Kings 9:36)
13. A ram (Genesis 22:13)
14. Horses of fire (2 Kings 2:24)

✦Snakes and Other Creepy Things

1. Who amazed his comrades by surviving the bite of a viper?
2. According to Proverbs, what substance affects man like the bite of a snake?
3. Who put a bronze snake on a pole in order to heal snakebite?
4. According to Job, what sort of men suck the poison of snakes?
5. What repulsive creatures bit the Israelites in the wilderness?
6. What did the people of Judah call the bronze snake in the temple?
7. What kind of snake did God promise to Jeremiah as a punishments for Israel's sin?
8. What tribe of Israel was supposed to be like a snake?
9. What animal came out of the Nile in droves as a plague on the Egyptians?
10. What bloodsucking creature is, in Proverbs, held us as an example of something that can never be satisfied?
11. According to Jesus, what would a loveless father give a child who asked for an egg?
12. What destructive creature did the prophet Joel have a vision of?
13. Who had a rod that God turned into a snake?
14. According to the Law, what hopping insects were edible?
15. What did King Rehoboam say he would use to discipline the people?
16. What book makes the pessimistic statement that whoever breaks through a wall may be bitten by a snake?
17. In Revelation, what sort of creatures had tails that were like snakes?

♦Snakes and Other Creepy Things (Answers)

1. Paul (Acts 28:3-6)
2. Wine (Proverbs 23:32)
3. Moses (Numbers 21:8-9)
4. The wicked (Job 20:16).
5. Fiery serpents (Numbers 21:6)
6. Nehushtan (2 Kings 18:4)
7. Vipers that could not be charmed (Jeremiah 8:17)
8. Dan (Genesis 49:17)
9. Frogs (Exodus 8:1-4)
10. The leech (Proverbs 30:15)
11. A scorpion (Luke 11:12)
12. The locust (Joel 1:1-4)
13. Moses (Exodus 4:3)
14. The locust and the grasshopper (Leviticus 11:22)
15. Scorpions (1 Kings 12:11, 14)
16. Ecclesiastes (10:8)
17. Horses (Revelation 9:19)

18. Who did Jesus refer to as a brood of vipers?
19. What was the only animal to lie?
20. In Revelation, what was the name of the great serpent?
21. According to Isaiah, what is the food of the serpent?
22. Who had a vision of locusts that were like horses prepared for battle?
23. Could the Israelites eat lizards?
24. According to Psalm 91, what kind of man can tread on a cobra without fear?
25. What did Amos say would happen to a man who rested his hand on the wall of his own house?
26. Who predicted that a child would be able to put his hand over a snake's den?
27. Who told his followers they would have the power to handle deadly snakes?
28. What curse did God put on the lying snakes?
29. What creature supposedly melts away as it moves?
30. What kind of tails did the hideous locusts have in Revelation?
31. What did the author of Proverbs admire the snake for?
32. According to Genesis, what part of man is the snake supposed to strike at?
33. What voracious insect was a plague on the Egyptians?
34. Who described locusts as stretching across the heavens like a dark curtain?
35. According to Ecclesiastes, what gives perfume a bad smell?
36. What prophet referred to the Sadducees and Pharisees as vipers?
37. What tiny insect did David compare himself to when Saul pursued him?
38. To what loathsome creature did Bildad compare man?
39. What swarming, pesky insects were sent as a plague on the Egyptians?
40. What ruler was eaten by worms before he died?

18. The scribes and Pharisees (Matthew 23:33)
19. The serpent (Genesis 3:1-13)
20. The Devil (Revelation 12:9)
21. Dust (Isaiah 65:25)
22. John (Revelation 9:7)
23. No (Leviticus 11:29)
24. The man who trusts God (verse 13)
25. A snake would bite him (Amos 5:19)
26. Isaiah (11:8)
27. Jesus (Mark 16:18)
28. It would have to crawl on its belly and eat dust (Genesis 3:14)
29. The slug (Psalm 58:8)
30. Tails like scorpions (Revelation 9:10)
31. Its grace of movement (Proverbs 30:19)
32. The heel (Genesis 3:15)
33. The locust (Exodus 10:12-19)
34. Isaiah (40:22)
35. Dead flies (Ecclesiastes 10:1)
36. John the Baptist (Matthew 3:7)
37. A flea (1 Samuel 24:14)
38. A worm (Job 25:6)
39. Gnats and flies (Exodus 8:16-32)
40. Herod (Acts 12:23)

41. According to Jesus, what insect devours the treasures we store up on earth?
42. What creature, according to Isaiah, will not die?
43. Who had a fly god named Baal-zebub?
44. Who ate locusts in the wilderness?
45. What stinging creature did God promise to protect Ezekiel from?
46. What prophet had his vine eaten by a worm?
47. What water creature is the Bible probably referring to when it talks about a dragon?
48. When Israel's spies came back from Canaan, what insect did they compare themselves to when describing the giants in the land?
49. In the Law, what mammal is classified as an unclean bird?
50. According to Jesus, what small insects are strained out by the Pharisees?
51. What industrious insect is held up as an example to the lazy man?
52. According to Bildad, what fragile thing is a godless man's trust like?
53. Who imitated Moses' feat of turning a staff into a snake?

✦A Den of Lions

1. What future king claimed that he had grabbed lions by the throat and beat them to death?
2. Who tore a lion apart with his bare hands?
3. Who saw locusts with lions' teeth?
4. What book speaks of the Lion of the Tribe of Judah?
5. What father and son did David say were stronger than lions?
6. According to 1 Peter, what person is like a ravenous lion?

41. The moth (Luke 12:33)
42. The worm (Isaiah 66:24)
43. The people of Ekron (2 Kings 1:2)
44. John the Baptist (Mark 1:6)
45. The scorpion (Ezekiel 2:6)
46. Jonah (4:7)
47. The crocodile
48. The grasshopper (Numbers 13:33)
49. The bat (Leviticus 11:19)
50. Gnats (Matthew 23:24)
51. The ant (Proverbs 6:6-8)
52. A spider web (Job 8:14)
53. The Egyptian court magicians (Exodus 7:11)

✦A Den of Lions (Answers)

1. David (1 Samuel 17:35)
2. Samson (Judges 14:6)
3. Joel (1:6)
4. Revelation (5:5)
5. Saul and Jonathan (2 Samuel 1:23)
6. Satan (1 Peter 5:8)

7. What brave soldier in David's army went into a pit on a snowy day and killed a lion?
8. Who had a throne with lion statues beside it?
9. What prophet foresaw a time when a lion would eat straw instead of meat?
10. Which of his sons did the dying Jacob compare to a vicious lion?
11. What prophet had a vision of a creature that had, on one of its four sides, a lion's face?
12. What devout young man was placed in a lions' den?
13. According to Ecclesiastes, what is better than being a dead lion?
14. Who saw a lionlike creature near the throne of God?
15. What book has a man asking his loved one to come down from the place where lions dwell?
16. Who had a vision of a lion with eagle's wings?

✦Shepherds and Sheep

1. What wealthy man had fourteen thousand sheep?
2. Who married the shepherd girl Zipporah?
3. What former shepherd boy is supposed to have written, "The Lord is my shepherd"?
4. Who did Jesus command to shepherd his church?
5. Who was the first shepherd?
6. Who is the good shepherd?
7. Which prophet said, "All we like sheep have gone astray"?
8. Which Old Testament book compares a lover's teeth to a flock of newly shorn sheep?
9. In which gospel does Jesus speak of separating the sheep from the goats?
10. Who had compassion on the people because they seemed like sheep without a shepherd?

7. Benaiah (2 Samuel 23:20)
8. Solomon (1 Kings 10:18-20)
9. Isaiah (11:7)
10. Judah (Genesis 49:9)
11. Ezekiel (1:10)
12. Daniel (6:16)
13. A live dog (Ecclesiastes 9:4)
14. John (Revelation 4:7)
15. The Song of Solomon (4:8)
16. Daniel (7:4)

◆Shepherds and Sheep (Answers)

1. Job (42:12)
2. Moses (Exodus 2:16-17)
3. David (Psalm 23:1)
4. Peter (John 21:15-17)
5. Abel (Genesis 4:2)
6. Jesus (John 10:11)
7. Isaiah (53:6)
8. The Song of Solomon (4:2)
9. Matthew (25:32)
10. Jesus (Matthew 9:36)

11. Who called Saul on the carpet because he had heard the bleating of sheep taken in Saul's battle with the Amalekites?

12. What book warns against sacrificing a defective sheep to God?

13. In what book does God say, "My people hath been lost sheep; their shepherds have caused them to go astray"?

14. To whom did Jesus say, "I send you forth as sheep in the midst of wolves"?

15. In Jesus' parable of the lost sheep, how many sheep were in the field?

16. Who did God tell Moses would be the new shepherd over Israel?

17. Which psalm says, "We are his people and the sheep of his pasture"?

18. Which epistle says, "We were as sheep going astray"?

19. Which psalm says, "We are counted as sheep for the slaughter"?

20. Who became a shepherd in Midian for his father-in-law?

21. Who paid Jesse a visit when young David was out tending the sheep?

22. What daughter of Laban was a shepherdess?

23. Who was out shearing his sheep when David's servants called on him?

24. What prophet said, "Woe to the idle shepherd"?

25. What prophet said that God would search out his scattered sheep?

26. What prophet told Ahab that Israel was scattered like sheep?

27. What Old Testament book says, "Smite the shepherd and the sheep will be scattered"?

28. According to Isaiah, whom did God say was his appointed shepherd?

29. Which epistle speaks of the "great shepherd of the sheep"?

11. Samuel (1 Samuel 15:14)
12. Deuteronomy (17:1)
13. Jeremiah (50:6)
14. The twelve disciples (Matthew 10:16)
15. A hundred (Matthew 18:12-14)
16. Joshua (Numbers 27:16-18)
17. 100
18. 1 Peter (2:25)
19. 44:22
20. Moses (Exodus 3:1)
21. Samuel (1 Samuel 16:11)
22. Rachel (Genesis 29:9)
23. Nabal (1 Samuel 25:2-9)
24. Zechariah (11:17)
25. Ezekiel (34:11)
26. Micaiah (1 Kings 22:17)
27. Zechariah (13:7)
28. Cyrus (Isaiah 44:28)
29. Hebrews (13:20)

30. What prophet talked about a shepherd pulling parts of a sheep from a lion's mouth?
31. In what book do we find the words, "He shall feed his flock like a shepherd"?
32. What almost-slaughtered son asked his father, "Where is the lamb for a burnt offering?"
33. Who said, "Behold, the lamb of God"?
34. What prophet told David a tale about a man with one lamb?
35. What foreign traveler was reading a passage about the Messiah being like a sheep for the slaughter?
36. What book of the Bible describes a lamb with seven horns and seven eyes?
37. What prophet spoke of a wolf dwelling with a lamb?
38. For what festival, instituted during the exodus from Egypt, was a lamb slaughtered?
39. Which epistle refers to Christ as a Passover lamb?
40. Who found a ram caught in a bramble?
41. Who had a vision of a powerful ram on a destructive rampage?
42. Who used a sheep's horn as a container for oil?
43. In front of what Canaanite city did priests blow trumpets made of rams' horns?
44. What did Samuel tell Saul was more important than sacrificing sheep?
45. What king of Moab was noted as a keeper of sheep?

◆Biblical Bird Walk

1. What book says that anyone who scorns his parents will have his eyes pecked out by ravens?
2. In Revelation, what bird went about crying, "Woe! Woe!"?
3. What book portrays God as having wings and feathers?

30. Amos (3:12)
31. Isaiah (40:11)
32. Isaac (Genesis 22:7)
33. John the Baptist (John 1:29)
34. Nathan (2 Samuel 12:1-7)
35. The Ethiopian eunuch (Acts 8:27-35)
36. Revelation (5:6)
37. Isaiah (11:6)
38. Passover (Exodus 12:21)
39. 1 Corinthians (5:7)
40. Abraham (Genesis 22:13)
41. Daniel (8:3-4)
42. Samuel (1 Samuel 16:1)
43. Jericho (Joshua 6:4)
44. Obeying God (1 Samuel 15:22)
45. Mesha (2 Kings 3:4)

✦Biblical Bird Walk (Answers)

1. Proverbs (30:17)
2. An eagle (Revelation 8:13)
3. Psalms (91:4)

4. What bird does the lover in Song of Solomon compare his beloved's eyes to?
5. What king instructed people in bird lore?
6. Who compared his days to eagles swooping down on their prey?
7. On what day did God create the birds?
8. Who had a dream about birds eating out of a basket on his head?
9. Who boasted to David that he would give David's body to the birds for food?
10. What king's search for his rival is compared with looking for a partridge in the mountains?
11. What bird in great droves fed the Israelites in the wilderness?
12. On Mount Sinai, God told Moses that he had carried the Israelites from Egypt on the wings of a bird. What bird?
13. What father and son were, according to David, swifter than eagles?
14. According to the Law, what must a Nazarite sacrifice if someone dies in his presence during his period of separation?
15. What prophet had a vision of a desolate day when no birds were in the sky?
16. In Ezekiel's vision of the creatures with four faces, what bird's face was on the creatures?
17. What Babylonian king had a dream of a tree where every bird found shelter?
18. Who had a vision of a lion with eagle's wings?
19. What prophet said that Ephraim was as easily deceived as a foolish dove?
20. What nation would, according to Obadiah, be brought down by God even though it had soared like an eagle?
21. Who had a vision of two women with storks' wings?
22. Who prophesied that Assyria would become a roosting place for all sorts of strange night birds?

4. The dove (Song of Solomon 1:15)
5. Solomon (1 Kings 4:33)
6. Job (9:26)
7. The fifth day (Genesis 1:20)
8. Pharaoh's baker (Genesis 40:16-17)
9. Goliath (1 Samuel 17:44)
10. Saul's search for David (1 Samuel 26:20)
11. Quails (Exodus 16:13)
12. The eagle (Exodus 19:4)
13. Saul and Jonathan (2 Samuel 1:23)
14. Two doves (Numbers 6:10)
15. Jeremiah (4:25)
16. The eagle's (Ezekiel 1:10)
17. Nebuchadnezzar (Daniel 4:12)
18. Daniel (7:4)
19. Hosea (7:11)
20. Edom (Obadiah 4)
21. Zechariah (5:9)
22. Zephaniah (2:14)

23. Who had a vision of a sheet filled with all sorts of unclean birds and other animals?
24. What domestic bird signaled Peter's betrayal of Christ?
25. According to Jesus, what inevitably gathers near a dead body?
26. What form did the Holy Spirit assume at Jesus' baptism?
27. In what parable of Jesus do greedy birds play a major role?
28. Who predicted that desert birds would use a ruined Edom as their home?
29. Who called his lover "my dove, my perfect one"?
30. Who warned people that the birds of the air could be tattletales, telling the king who had said bad things about him?
31. In Revelation, who told the birds to gather together to eat the flesh of warriors?
32. According to Psalm 147, what young birds are fed by God when they call to him?
33. What prophet said that God's protection for Jerusalem was like birds circling overhead?
34. According to Leviticus, what must be done to any bird killed for food?
35. According to the Law, what two types of birds comprise the category of unclean fowl?
36. How many of each species of bird was Noah supposed to take into the ark?
37. Who had a vision of a woman with eagle's wings flying to the desert?
38. According to James, what cannot be tamed even though all birds can be tamed?
39. Who said that idolatrous man had exchanged the glory of the true God for images like birds?
40. What bird was being sold in the temple courts when Jesus drove out the salesmen?
41. What bird, according to Jesus, is cared for by God even though it had no barns or store rooms?

23. Peter (Acts 10:9-13)
24. The rooster (John 13:38; 18:27)
25. Vultures (Luke 17:37)
26. A dove (Mark 1:10)
27. The parable of the sower (Mark 4:1-20)
28. Isaiah (34:11-14)
29. The lover in the Song of Solomon (6:9)
30. The author of Ecclesiastes (10:20)
31. An angel standing in the sun (Revelation 19:17)
32. Ravens (verse 9)
33. Isaiah (31:5)
34. The blood must be drained from it (Leviticus 17:13)
35. Mostly scavengers and birds of prey (Deuteronomy 14:12-18)
36. Seven (Genesis 7:3)
37. John (Revelation (12:14)
38. The tongue (James 3:7)
39. Paul (Romans 1:23)
40. Doves (John 2:14)
41. The raven (Luke 12:24)

42. What kind of bird did Jesus compare to his love for Jerusalem?

43. What prophet warned of a destruction in which all birds would be swept from the earth?

44. What prophet warned that he would wail like an owl and walk about barefoot and naked?

45. Who declared that Nineveh's slave girls would moan like doves when the city was plundered?

46. In what book does God say that he knows all the birds of the air and the beasts of the field?

47. According to Job, what is hidden from the keen-eyed birds of prey?

48. What beautiful bird did Solomon's navy bring to Israel?

49. When the king of Syria besieged Samaria, what unusual substance sold for five shekels in the city?

50. What prophet said that Ahab's people would be eaten by birds?

51. According to Psalm 68, what are the dove's feathers covered with?

52. Who said that he had become a companion of owls?

53. According to Psalm 84, what two small birds have a nesting place near the temple?

54. What bird's song is, in the Song of Solomon, a sign of spring?

55. What bird's youth is, according to Psalms, renewable?

56. What bird does Jeremiah compare to a man who gains riches by unjust means?

57. According to Ezekiel, what will the moaning of the survivors sound like?

58. In what book do you find this: "Mine enemies chased me sore, like a bird, without cause"?

59. What was the first bird released from the ark?

60. In the system of sacrifice, what bird was normally offered?

61. What means did the Lord use to bring quail to the Israelites?

42. A hen gathering her chicks (Matthew 23:37)
43. Zephaniah (1:3)
44. Micah (1:8)
45. Nahum (2:7)
46. Psalms (50:11)
47. The whereabouts of jewels and precious metal (Job 28:7)
48. The peacock (2 Chronicles 9:21—some modern translations have "ape" instead of "peacock.")
49. Dove's dung (2 Kings 6:25)
50. Elijah (1 Kings 21:24)
51. Gold (Psalm 68:13)
52. Job (30:29)
53. The sparrow and the swallow (Psalm 84:3)
54. The turtledove (Song of Solomon 2:12)
55. The eagle (Psalm 103:5)
56. A partridge that hatches eggs it does not lay (Jeremiah 17:11)
57. Doves (Ezekiel 7:16)
58. Lamentations (3:52)
59. A raven (Genesis 8:7)
60. A dove or pigeon (Leviticus 1:14-17)
61. A wind from the sea (Numbers 11:31)

62. What concubine of Saul stood by the unburied bodies of her sons in order to keep the birds away?

63. According to the Law, one of the curses of disobedience was the coming of a cruel nation. What bird is that nation compared to?

64. According to the Law, what is an Israelite to do if he finds a mother bird with young or with eggs?

65. What was the dove carrying in its beak when it returned to Noah?

66. Who, according to tradition, said, "Oh, that I had the wings of a dove"?

67. Who asked Job who provided for the feeding of young ravens?

68. According to the Bible, what foolish bird lays its eggs on the ground in the sun?

69. What psalm speaks of the quail the Israelites ate in the wilderness?

70. What king always had choice poultry in his daily provisions?

71. Who did God tell to have dominion over all the birds?

72. What greedy king does Isaiah compare to a man grabbing eggs from a bird's nest?

73. What black birds fed Elijah when he lived by Kerith Brook?

74. According to Job, what bird feeds blood to its young?

75. What prophet told Baasha, king of Israel, that the birds would feast on those of his household?

76. What bird does Proverbs compare fleeting riches to?

77. What book speaks of the uselessness of spreading out a net in view of the birds it is supposed to catch?

78. According to the Song of Solomon, what is the male lover's hair like?

79. What nation's women did Isaiah compare to fluttering birds?

80. What book says that the Lord's people have become as heartless as ostriches in the desert?

62. Rizpah (2 Samuel 21:10)
63. An eagle (Deuteronomy 28:49)
64. He may take the young or the eggs, but must not kill the mother bird (Deuteronomy 22:6-7)
65. An olive leaf (Genesis 8:11)
66. David (Psalm 55:6)
67. God (Job 38:41)
68. The ostrich (Job 39:13-18—some translations have "stork")
69. 78:26-29
70. Solomon (1 Kings 4:23)
71. Noah (Genesis 9:1-7)
72. The king of Assyria (Isaiah 10:14)
73. Ravens (1 Kings 17:6)
74. The eagle (Job 39:30)
75. Jehu (1 Kings 16:4)
76. An eagle (Proverbs 23:5)
77. Proverbs (1:17)
78. A raven (Song of Solomon 5:11)
79. Moab's (Isaiah 16:2)
80. Lamentations (4:3)

81. Who told the Moabites to live like doves nesting at the mouth of a cave?

82. According to Isaiah, from what direction does God summon the birds of prey?

83. Who compared Assyria with a cedar of Lebanon that sheltered all the birds in its branches?

84. Who compared Israel with a speckled bird of prey, surrounded and attacked by other birds of prey?

85. According to Isaiah, what will those who hope in the Lord fly like?

86. According to Jeremiah, what large bird knows it has appointed seasons?

87. What prophet asked, "Does a bird fall into a trap on the ground where no snare has been set"? (NIV)

88. According to Jesus, what does not sow nor reap?

89. What seed grows a plant so large that the birds can make nests in it?

90. What did Mary and Joseph sacrifice in the temple when they took the young Jesus there?

91. In John's vision of the four living creatures, what bird does one of the creatures resemble?

92. According to the law, what can be used in place of a lamb as a sin offering?

93. What two birds did Abram sacrifice to God?

94. What prayer of an afflicted man compares him to an owl living among ruins?

95. According to Psalm 104, what bird nests in the pine trees?

96. According to Proverbs, what is an undeserved curse like?

97. What city, according to John, will become a home for every detestable and unclean bird?

98. What book says that in old age the songs of the birds will grow faint?

99. According to Isaiah, what bird honors God for providing streams in the desert?

100. What prophet speaks of God's covenant with the birds of the air?

81. Jeremiah (48:28)
82. The east (Isaiah 46:11)
83. Ezekiel (31:6)
84. Jeremiah (12:9)
85. Eagles (Isaiah 40:31)
86. The stork (Jeremiah 8:7)
87. Amos (3:5)
88. The birds of the air (Matthew 6:26)
89. The mustard seed (Luke 13:18-19)
90. A pair of doves (Luke 2:24)
91. An eagle (Revelation 4:7)
92. Two doves (Leviticus 5:7)
93. A dove and a pigeon (Genesis 15:9)
94. Psalm 102:6
95. The stork (verse 17)
96. A fluttering sparrow or swallow (Proverbs 26:2)
97. Babylon (Revelation 18:2)
98. Ecclesiastes (12:4)
99. The owl (Isaiah 43:20)
100. Hosea (2:18)

✦The Lowly Donkey

1. What prophet of Moab had a talking donkey?
2. What future king was looking for lost donkeys when he ran into Samuel?
3. Who gave his irate brother twenty donkeys as a goodwill gesture?
4. What prince was riding a mule (that's a half-donkey) when he got his head caught in an oak tree?
5. Who took his wife and sons and set them on a donkey when he returned to Egypt, his boyhood home?
6. What future wife of David rode out to meet him on a donkey when she was pleading for her husband's life?
7. Who used a donkey to carry the wood he was using to sacrifice his son on?
8. Who sent her servant on a donkey to inform Elisha that her son had died?
9. What prophet predicted that the Messiah would enter in riding on a donkey?
10. What is the only gospel to mention Jesus' riding on a donkey?

✦Horses and Horsemen

1. What book of the Old Testament contains a hymn celebrating drowned horses?
2. What New Testament author had a vision of locusts that looked like horses?
3. What evil queen was executed by Jerusalem's Horse Gate?
4. What leader was told by God to cripple his enemies' horses?
5. What king had twelve thousand cavalry horses?
6. What king took his household manager out to look for grass for the royal horses?

✦The Lowly Donkey (Answers)

1. Balaam (Numbers 22:21-33)
2. Saul (1 Samuel 9:1-6)
3. Jacob (Genesis 32:13-18)
4. Absalom (2 Samuel 18:9)
5. Moses (Exodus 4:20)
6. Abigail (1 Samuel 25:20)
7. Abraham (Genesis 22:1-3)
8. The Shunemite woman (2 Kings 4:18-32)
9. Zechariah (9:9)
10. Matthew (21:1-9)

✦Horses and Horsemen (Answers)

1. Exodus (chapter 15, Miriam's song)
2. John (Revelation 9:7)
3. Athaliah (2 Chronicles 23:15)
4. Joshua (11:6)
5. Solomon (1 Kings 4:26)
6. Ahab (1 Kings 18:5)

7. What two prophets were separated by horses of fire?
8. What queen had her blood spattered on King Jehu's horses?
9. Who removed the horse idols that the kings of Judah had dedicated to the worship of the sun?
10. What prophet had a vision of locusts that run like war horses?
11. Who had a vision of an angel on a red horse?
12. What king had horses imported from Cilicia and Musri?
13. Who ordered seventy horsemen to accompany Paul out of Jerusalem?
14. Who had a vision of the hills filled with horses and chariots of fire?
15. What prophet saw four chariots pulled by horses that represented the four winds?
16. In Revelation, what horse represents Death?
17. Who had horsemen accompany him as he went to bury his father?

7. Elijah and Elisha (2 Kings 2:11)
8. Jezebel (2 Kings 9:33)
9. Josiah (2 Kings 23:11)
10. Joel (2:4)
11. Zechariah (1:8)
12. Solomon (1 Kings 10:29)
13. Claudius Lysias (Acts 23:23)
14. Elisha's servant (2 Kings 6:17)
15. Zechariah (6:1-5)
16. The pale horse (Revelation 6:8)
17. Joseph (Genesis 50:9)

PART 2
The Great Outdoors

✦The Biblical Greenhouse

1. What plant sprang up miraculously to give shade to the prophet Jonah?
2. What woman used mandrakes to gain a night in bed with Jacob?
3. Who used rods of poplar, hazel, and chestnut trees to make genetic changes in his cattle?
4. What kind of tree did the weary Elijah sit under?
5. What plant had such a bitter taste that it became a symbol for sorrow and disaster?
6. What, according to the New Testament, produces the smallest seed of any plant?
7. Which book mentions the rose of Sharon and the lily of the valley?
8. What mythical creature eats grass—according to the Book of Job?
9. What is the only book of the Bible to mention the apple tree?
10. What kind of tree did Zacchaeus climb in order to see Jesus?
11. What tree was a symbol of grace, elegance, and uprightness?
12. What kind of wood was Noah's ark made of?
13. What miraculous event was the eating of bitter herbs supposed to commemorate?
14. What unusual food was said to have resembled coriander seed?
15. What tree's spice was used in making oil for anointing?

✦The Biblical Greenhouse (Answers)

1. A gourd (Jonah 4:6)
2. Leah (Genesis 30:14-16)
3. Jacob (Genesis 30:37-39)
4. A broom tree (1 Kings 19:4)
5. Wormwood (Proverbs 5:4; Amos 5:7)
6. Mustard (Matthew 13:31)
7. Song of Solomon (2:1)
8. Behemoth (Job 40:15-22)
9. Song of Solomon (2:3)
10. A sycamore (Luke 19:1-4)
11. The palm (Psalm 92:12; Jeremiah 10:5)
12. Gopherwood (Genesis 6:14)
13. The Passover (Exodus 12:8)
14. Manna (Exodus 16:31)
15. The cassia tree (Exodus 30:24)

16. What grain did not suffer from the plague of hail in Egypt because it had not grown enough?
17. What did Jacob send as a gift to Joseph in Egypt?
18. What massive trees were brought to make the beams and pillars in the Jerusalem temple?
19. What expensive wood is mentioned in the Book of Revelation?
20. What vine is mentioned in the Old Testament as bearing poisonous berries?
21. What kind of tree does Psalms compare a wicked man to?
22. What prophet complained about the people making sacrifices under spreading oaks, poplars, and elms?
23. What kind of weed does Jesus say will be separated from the wheat at the last judgment?
24. What kind of wood was the ark of the covenant made of?
25. What prophet was a "dresser of sycamore trees"?
26. What kind of trees did the exiled Jews hang their harps upon?
27. What did Delilah use to bind the sleeping Samson?
28. What defeated king was buried with his sons under an oak tree?
29. Which tree does Jesus say can be uprooted and thrown into the sea—if one has enough faith?
30. What city was the "city of palm trees"?
31. What tree's foliage was found in the carvings inside the temple?
32. What king appointed an overseer to watch after the fruits of the olive trees and sycamores?
33. Who was killed after his hair was caught in an oak's branches?
34. What man met the Lord at the oaks of Mamre?
35. What prophet had a vision of a branch of an almond tree?
36. To what king did Jesus compare the lilies of the field?
37. What plant was used to purify lepers?

16. Rye (Exodus 9:32)
17. Almonds (Genesis 43:11)
18. The cedars of Lebanon (1 Kings 5:6)
19. Thyine (Revelation 18:12)
20. The vine of Sodom (Deuteronomy 32:32)
21. A green bay tree (Psalm 37:35)
22. Hosea (4:13)
23. Tares (Matthew 13:25)
24. Acacia (Exodus 25:10)
25. Amos (7:14)
26. Willows (Psalms 137:2)
27. "Green withs"—probably tree bark or twigs (Judges 16:11)
28. Saul (1 Chronicles 10:12)
29. The sycamine (Luke 17:6)
30. Jericho (2 Chronicles 28:15)
31. The palm (1 Kings 6:29)
32. David (1 Chronicles 27:28)
33. Absalom (2 Samuel 18:9-10)
34. Abraham (Genesis 18:1)
35. Jeremiah (1:11)
36. Solomon (Luke 12:27)
37. Hyssop (Leviticus 14:4-6)

38. When Rahab hid the Israelite spies on her rooftop, what did she hide them under?

39. What did Noah's dove bring back in its beak?

40. What kind of tree was withered by Jesus because it bore no fruit?

41. What tree's leaves were used to cover the naked Adam and Eve?

42. What tree's fruit was used to make a plaster to heal the diseased King Hezekiah?

43. What furnishings in the temple were made of olive wood?

44. What epistle uses the grafting of the olive tree as a symbol of God choosing the Gentiles in addition to the Jews?

45. What prophet mentions a gift of ebony wood sent to Tyre?

46. In what land did Moses see a burning bush that was not consumed?

47. On what day of Creation did God make the plants?

48. What kind of flowers were supposed to be carved into the sacred lampstands?

49. What were Solomon's chariots made of?

50. What book mentions "apples of gold"?

51. In the parable of the sower, what unwanted plant causes some of the seeds to die?

52. What was Moses' basket made of?

53. What plant was used to lift up a sponge to the dying Jesus?

54. What plant was given to Jesus as a mock scepter by the Roman soldiers?

55. What plant food, given to pigs, was wanted by the prodigal son?

56. What flower were the capitals on the temple columns shaped like?

57. What plant, according to Isaiah, would not be broken by the Messiah?

58. What tree's fruit was symbolically represented on the clothing of Israel's high priest?

38. Stacks of flax (Joshua 2:6)
39. An olive twig (Genesis 8:11)
40. A fig tree (Mark 11:12-14)
41. The fig's (Genesis 3:7)
42. The fig's (2 Kings 20:7)
43. The cherubim (1 Kings 6:23)
44. Romans (11:17)
45. Ezekiel (27:15)
46. Midian (Exodus 3:2)
47. The third day (Genesis 1:9-13)
48. Almond blossoms (Exodus 25:33)
49. Cedar wood (Song of Solomon 3:9)
50. Proverbs (25:11)
51. Thorns (Matthew 13:7)
52. Bulrushes (Exodus 2:3)
53. Hyssop (John 19:29)
54. A reed (Mark 15:19)
55. Pods (Luke 15:16)
56. Lilies (1 Kings 7:19)
57. A bruised reed (Isaiah 42:3)
58. The pomegranate's (Exodus 28:33)

59. What leaves were thrown down in front of Jesus on his entry into Jerusalem?

60. What wood was used to make the table in the tabernacle for holding the sacred bread?

61. What wood was used for building the temple after the exile in Babylon?

62. What two herbs does Jesus say the Pharisees would tithe?

◆Some Earthquakes

1. What famous mountain smoked like a furnace and quaked greatly?

2. An earthquake at Philippi eventually led to the release of two Christians from prison there. Who were they?

3. Which Gospel mentions an earthquake in connection with the Resurrection of Jesus?

4. An earthquke during King Uzziah's reign was so remarkable that one of the Hebrew prophets dates his book "two years before the earthquake." Which prophet?

5. According to Matthew's Gospel, an earthquke occurred when Jesus died on the cross. What other spectacular event occurred at that time in the temple?

6. What Hebrew prophet experienced an earthquake, a strong wind, and a supernatural fire all in one day?

7. During Saul's reign an earthquake occurred during the attack on the Philistines at Michmash. Who led the attack?

8. During a rebellion under Moses, 250 people rebelled and were swallowed up in an earthquake. Who led the rebellion?

59. Palm leaves (John 12:13)
60. Acacia (Exodus 25:23-30)
61. Cedar (Ezra 3:7)
62. Mint and rue (Luke 11:42)

✦Some Earthquakes (Answers)

1. Sinai (Exodus 19:17, 18)
2. Paul and Silas (Acts 16:25-27)
3. Matthew (28:2)
4. Amos (1:1)
5. The temple veil (curtain) was torn in half from top to bottom (Matthew 27:51)
6. Elijah (1 Kings 19:9-12)
7. Jonathan (1 Samuel 14:15)
8. Korah (Numbers 16:31-33)

◆Blowing in the Wind

1. What Old Testament book speaks of life as a "chasing after the wind"?
2. Where were the disciples when they heard a noise that sounded like a mighty wind filling the house they had gathered in?
3. Who had a dream of seven heads of grain being scorched by a hot east wind?
4. What loathsome creatures did God drive into Egypt with an east wind?
5. What prophet was told to cut off his hair and scatter a third of it in the wind?
6. How long did the wind that parted the Red Sea blow?
7. According to James, what sort of person is like a wave tossed by the wind?
8. What prophet experienced a furious wind that split the hills and shattered the rocks?
9. Whose children were destroyed when a strong wind struck the house they were banqueting in?
10. According to the Book of Job, what directional wind will inevitably strike down the wicked?
11. What epistle compares false teachers to rainless clouds blown about by the wind?
12. According to Psalms, what sort of people are like chaff that the wind blows away?
13. Who did God address from a whirlwind?
14. According to Jesus, what sort of man sees his house fall when the winds beat against it?
15. What was blown out of Egypt by a strong west wind?
16. Who had a dream about a statue that crumbled into dust that was driven away by the wind?
17. What prophet spoke of people who sow a wind and reap a whirlwind?
18. What runaway boarded a ship that the Lord struck with a strong wind?

✦Blowing in the Wind (Answers)

1. Ecclesiastes (chapters 1 and 2)
2. Jerusalem (Acts 2:2)
3. Pharaoh (Genesis 41:6)
4. Locusts (Exodus 10:13)
5. Ezekiel (5:2)
6. All night (Exodus 14:21)
7. A doubter (James 1:6)
8. Elijah (1 Kings 19:11)
9. Job's (Job 1:19)
10. East (Job 27:21)
11. Jude (12)
12. The wicked (Psalm 1:4)
13. Job (38:1)
14. The foolish man who builds on the sand (Matthew 7:26-27)
15. Locusts (Exodus 10:19)
16. Nebuchadnezzar (Daniel 2:35)
17. Hosea (8:7)
18. Jonah (1:4)

19. What prophet suffered from a hot east wind after his shade plant was eaten by a worm?
20. Who lost faith and began to flounder when he noticed the strong wind on a lake?
21. Who was saved from being a full-time sailor when God sent a wind to dry up the flood waters?
22. What food did God bring to the Israelites by using a wind?
23. According to the Book of Job, which directional wind punishes the land with its heat?
24. According to Revelation, what sort of creatures held back the winds from blowing on the earth?
25. What prophet had a vision of the four winds lashing the surface of the oceans?
26. In what book does a woman call on the north wind and south wind to blow on her garden?
27. According to Proverbs, what kind of woman is as hard to restrain as the wind itself?

✦Under a Cloud

1. What two long-dead men were with Jesus when a shining cloud covered them?
2. What sign did God set in the clouds to indicate that he would never again flood the world?
3. Did the pillar of cloud in the wilderness lead the Israelites by day or by night?
4. What prophet saw a little cloud like a man's hand?
5. What epistle talks about a "cloud of witnesses"?
6. At what critical spot did the pillar of cloud separate the Egyptians from the Israelites?
7. What epistle mentions believers being caught up in the clouds to meet the Lord?
8. According to Jesus, what person will appear coming in glory on the clouds of heaven?

19. Jonah (4:8)
20. Peter (Matthew 14:30)
21. Noah (Genesis 8:1)
22. Quails (Numbers 11:31)
23. South (Job 37:17)
24. Four angels (Revelation 7:1)
25. Daniel (7:2)
26. Song of Solomon (4:16)
27. A nagging wife (Proverbs 27:16)

✦Under a Cloud (Answers)

1. Moses and Elijah (Matthew 17:5)
2. The rainbow (Genesis 9:13)
3. By day (Exodus 13:21-22)
4. Elijah (1 Kings 18:44)
5. Hebrews (12:1)
6. By the Red Sea (Exodus 14:20)
7. 1 Thessalonians (4:17)
8. The Son of man (Matthew 24:30)

9. In Revelation, what two unfortunate men are raised by God and then taken to heaven in a cloud?
10. On what mountain did God appear in the form of a cloud?
11. What object of the Israelites was notable for having the cloud of God's glory upon it?
12. What king, seeing the cloud in the temple, said that God had chosen to live in clouds and darkness?
13. What portable object did the cloud of God's glory appear over?
14. What epistle compares false teachers to clouds that bring no rain?
15. At what event did a cloud hide Jesus from the apostles' sight?
16. According to Zephaniah, what special day will be a day of clouds and blackness?

✦Rivers, Brooks, Lakes, Seas

1. What body of water was the first victim of the plague in Egypt?
2. What river did the Israelites cross when they entered Canaan?
3. What are the four rivers connected with the garden of Eden?
4. According to the Song of Solomon, what is so powerful that rivers cannot quench it?
5. Who lived by Kerith Brook?
6. Who proclaimed a fast at the river Ahava?
7. Who had a dream about cows standing by the riverside?
8. Who spoke of a river flowing with honey?
9. According to God's covenant with Abraham, how far did Abraham's land extend?
10. Who ordered the casting of the Israelite boys into the river?

9. The two witnesses (Revelation 11:12)
10. Sinai (Exodus 19:9)
11. The tabernacle (Exodus 40:34)
12. Solomon (1 Kings 8:10-11)
13. The ark of the covenant (Leviticus 16:2)
14. Jude (verse 12)
15. The Ascension (Acts 1:9)
16. The day of the Lord (Zephaniah 1:15)

✦Rivers, Brooks, Lakes, Seas (Answers)

1. The Nile (Exodus 7:7-15)
2. The Jordan (Joshua 1:1-2)
3. Gihon, Pison, Tigris, and Euphrates (Genesis 2:10-14)
4. Love (Song of Solomon 8:7)
5. Elijah (1 Kings 17:1-4)
6. Ezra (8:21)
7. The Pharaoh (Genesis 41:3)
8. Zophar (Job 20:17)
9. From the river of Egypt to the Euphrates (Genesis 15:18)
10. Pharaoh (Exodus 1:22)

11. In John's vision, what caused a third of the rivers on earth to become bitter?
12. What lake is called the Salt Sea in Genesis 14:3?
13. What apostle noted that he had been endangered by the sea and by rivers?
14. Who prophesied to the Jews by the Kebar River?
15. Who had a vision of a river of fire?
16. Who spoke about justice rolling down like a river?
17. Where did John baptize the repentant people?
18. What Christian woman worshiped with a group that met by a river?
19. In John's vision, what happened to the sea when the second angel poured out his bowl on it?
20. Who found a baby while down by the riverside?
21. By what river did Nebuchadnezzar defeat Pharaoh Neco of Egypt?
22. Who had a vision of a deep river that could not be passed over?
23. Who spoke of the Lord being displeased with "ten thousand rivers of oil"?
24. In Revelation, what is the fiery lake composed of?
25. Who fled across Kidron Brook to escape from Absalom?
26. Where were Pharaoh and his men drowned?
27. In Revelation, where does the pure river of the water of life flow out from?
28. According to James, what kind of man is like the waves of the sea?
29. Who lodged at the home of a tanner who lived by the sea?
30. What name is the Sea of Galilee called in the Gospel of John?
31. What were the seafaring east of Israel known as?
32. What was the Mediterranean usually called in Bible times?
33. What was the Sea of Galilee called in Old Testament times?
34. What happens to the sea in the world to come?

11. A star (Revelation 8:10-11)
12. The Dead Sea.
13. Paul (2 Corinthians 11:26)
14. Ezekiel (1:1)
15. Daniel (7:10)
16. Amos (5:24)
17. In the Jordan (Mark 1:5)
18. Lydia (Acts 16:13-14)
19. It turned to blood (Revelation 16:3)
20. Pharaoh's daughter (Exodus 2:5)
21. The Euphrates (Jeremiah 46:2)
22. Ezekiel (47:5)
23. Micah (6:7)
24. Burning sulfur (Revelation 19:20)
25. David (2 Samuel 15:13-23)
26. The Red Sea (Exodus 15:4)
27. The throne of God (Revelation 22:1)
28. A doubting man (James 1:6)
29. Peter (Acts 10:6)
30. The Sea of Tiberias (John 6:1)
31. The Philistines.
32. The Great Sea.
33. The Sea of Chinnereth.
34. It does not exist (Revelation 21:1)

35. Who had a vision of a sea of glass?
36. Who asked his shipmates to cast him into the sea?
37. By what lake did Jesus appear to his disciples after the Resurrection?
38. By what other name is the Salt Sea (Dead Sea) known in the Old Testament?
39. What Syrian army man had his leprosy washed away in the Jordan River?

✦From the Mountains

1. On what mountain did Elijah challenge the priests of Baal?
2. What mountain did Balaam plan to curse Israel from?
3. What mountain did Moses see the promised land from?
4. What mountain did Deborah and Barak descend to defeat Sisera?
5. Where did Noah's ark land?
6. Where did Jesus' Transfiguration occur?
7. Where did the Samaritans build their temple?
8. Where did Moses see the burning bush?
9. On what mountain did Solomon build the temple?
10. Where did Jesus weep over Jerusalem?
11. What mountain range did the wood for Solomon's temple come from?
12. Where were Saul and Jonathan killed by the Philistines?
13. Where was Moses buried?
14. Where did Jacob and Laban make their covenant?
15. Where did Elijah go when he fled from Jezebel?
16. Where did Aaron die?
17. Where did Abraham take Isaac to be sacrificed?
18. Where did Moses bring water out of the rock?
19. What mountain did David cross on his flight from Absalom?

35. John (Revelation 4:6)
36. Jonah (1:12)
37. The Sea of Tiberias (John 21:1)
38. The Sea of the Arabah.
39. Naaman (2 Kings 5:10-14)

✦From the Mountains (Answers)

1. Carmel (1 Kings 18:19)
2. Pisgah (Numbers 22-24)
3. Nebo (Deuteronomy 34:1-4)
4. Tabor (Judges 4:6-15)
5. Ararat (Genesis 8:4)
6. Harmon (Matthew 17)
7. Gerizim (John 4:20-21)
8. Horeb (Exodus 3:1)
9. Moriah (2 Chronicles 3:1)
10. The Mount of Olives (Luke 19:41)
11. Lebanon (1 Kings 5:6-14)
12. Gilboa (1 Samuel 31:1-6)
13. Pisgah (Deuteronomy 34:5-6)
14. Gilead (Genesis 31:20-49)
15. Horeb (1 Kings 19:8)
16. Mount Hor (Numbers 20:25-29)
17. Moriah (Genesis 22:2)
18. Horeb (Exodus 17:6)
19. The Mount of Olives. (2 Samuel 15:30-32)

20. What mountain in Jerusalem is mentioned over 160 times in the Bible?
21. On what smoke-covered mountain did Moses meet God?
22. What leader built an altar on Mount Ebal?
23. What prophet criticized the people who felt secure on Mount Samaria?
24. Where did Jesus deliver his final discourse?
25. In what country is Mount Seir?
26. According to Paul, what country is the site of Mount Sinai?

20. Zion
21. Sinai (Exodus 31:18)
22. Joshua (8:30)
23. Amos (6:1)
24. The Mount of Olives (Matthew 24-25)
25. Edom (Ezekiel 35:1-7)
26. Arabia (Galatians 4:25)

PART 3
Cities and Other Constructions

✦Cities Great And Small

1. What city, a seaport on the western coast of Asia Minor, was the second of the seven churches mentioned by John?
2. What city was Paul's hometown?
3. To what city in Macedonia did Paul send at least two letters?
4. What Asian city was the home of Lydia?
5. What city on the Euphrates did Abram leave?
6. What Canaanite city, destroyed by the Israelites has a name that means "ruin"?
7. What Pisidian city was visited by Paul and Barnabas on the first missionary journey?
8. In what city were the followers of Jesus first called Christians?
9. In what Italian city was Paul met by Christians from Rome?
10. What city is usually mentioned as the southern limit of Israel?
11. In what Greek city did Silas and Timothy stay while Paul went on to Athens?
12. What city was home to Mary, Martha, and Lazarus?
13. What city was the site of Jacob's famous dream?
14. What city was the birthplace of both David and Jesus?
15. What seaport in Asia did Paul walk to from Troas?
16. In what city did Paul address some of the most brilliant men of his time?
17. What famous city had Nebuchadnezzar as a ruler?
18. What Israelite city was built by Omri as his capital?

✦Cities Great And Small (Answers)

1. Smyrna (Revelation 2:8-11)
2. Tarsus (Acts 21:39)
3. Thessalonica.
4. Thyatira (Acts 16:14)
5. Ur (Genesis 15:7)
6. Ai (Joshua 8:3-29)
7. Antioch (Acts 13:14)
8. Antioch of Syria (Acts 11:26)
9. Appii Forum (Acts 28:15)
10. Beersheba.
11. Berea (Acts 17:10-14)
12. Bethany (John 11)
13. Bethel (Genesis 28:10-22)
14. Bethlehem.
15. Assos (Acts 20:13-14)
16. Athens (Acts 17)
17. Babylon (2 Kings 25)
18. Samaria (1 Kings 16:23-24)

19. What Asian city was the fifth of the seven churches mentioned by John?
20. In what Canaanite city were Joseph's bones finally laid to rest?
21. What city was the home of Peter, Andrew, and Philip?
22. Where was Cornelius converted?
23. Near what city did Peter profess his faith in Jesus?
24. Where did Jesus perform his first miracle?
25. Where did Jesus stay when John the Baptist was in prison?
26. What city was home to Philemon?
27. What sinful Greek city had a church that received two letters from Paul
28. In what Syrian city did Paul have his sight restored at the hands of Ananias?
29. What city, usually grouped with Iconium and Lystra, did Paul visit on his first and third missionary journeys?
30. What Asian city did Paul avoid so he could hurry back to Jerusalem?
31. What ancient city is associated wtih Joshua and the blowing of trumpets?
32. Where did Jonah board a ship bound for Tarshish?
33. What was Solomon's seaport at the head of the Gulf of Elath?
34. What Philistine city was home to Goliath?
35. What Philistine city did Amos curse for its slave trade with Edom?
36. Where did Solomon have a dream when he asked for wisdom?
37. Where did Abram go after leaving Ur?
38. What city, identified with Mamre, was the place where Sarah died?
39. In what Asian city did Paul and Barnabas make many converts on the second missionary journey?
40. Where were Paul and Barnabas deserted by Mark?
41. What city was said by John to have "Satan's seat"?

19. Sardis (Revelation 3:1-6)
20. Shechem (Joshua 24:32)
21. Bethsaida (John 1)
22. Caesarea (Acts 10:24-48)
23. Caesarea Philippi (Matthew 16:13-18)
24. Cana (John 2:1-11)
25. Capernaum (Matthew 4:12-13)
26. Colossae (Colossians 4:9)
27. Corinth.
28. Damascus (Acts 9)
29. Derbe (Acts 14:20)
30. Ephesus (Acts 19)
31. Jericho (Joshua 6)
32. Joppa (Jonah 1:3)
33. Ezion-Geber (1 Kings 9:26)
34. Gath (1 Samuel 17:4)
35. Gaza (Amos 1:6-7)
36. Gibeon (1 Kings 3:5-15)
37. Haran (Genesis 12)
38. Hebron (Genesis 23)
39. Iconium (Acts 13-14)
40. Perga (Acts 13:13-14)
41. Pergamos (Revelation 2:13)

42. What city receives most praise of all the seven cities of Asia?

43. Where did Paul and Silas make their first European converts?

44. Where was Paul's longest epistle sent?

45. Where did Assyrian king Sennacherib receive tribute from Hezekiah?

46. What city was said to have Christians that were neither hot nor cold?

47. Where was Paul mistaken for the god Hermes?

48. Where was King Josiah killed?

49. Where did Paul bid farewell to the elders of Ephesus?

50. What was Jesus' hometown?

51. What port was the site of Paul's first European landing?

52. What city was, according to tradition, founded by Nimrod?

53. What city of Cyprus did Paul and Barnabas visit on their first journey?

54. In what city did Paul, on his way to Jerusalem, board a ship sailing for Phoenicia?

55. What two cities of the plain were destroyed by God for their wickedness?

56. According to the New Testament, in what city will there be no night?

57. What city was Melchizedek king of?

58. Where did tax collector Zacchaeus live?

59. Where did Peter have his vision of a sheet filled with unclean animals?

60. What city is often referred to simply as Zion?

61. What was Jeremiah's hometown?

62. When the captive Paul was taken from Jerusalem to Caesarea, where did his guards stop for the night?

63. What city was home to the harlot Rahab?

64. At what town was Saul publicly proclaimed king?

65. In what Syrian city did Elisha visit a sick king?

66. What city was home to Philemon and Onesimus?

42. Philadelphia (Revelation 3:7-13)
43. Philippi (Acts 16)
44. Rome.
45. Lachish (2 Kings 18:13-16)
46. Laodicea (Revelation 3:14-22)
47. Lystra (Acts 14:6-20)
48. Megiddo (2 Kings 23:29)
49. Miletus (Acts 20:17-38)
50. Nazareth (Luke 2:51)
51. Neapolis (Acts 16:11)
52. Nineveh (Genesis 10:11)
53. Paphos (Acts 13:6-13)
54. Patara (Acts 21:1-20)
55. Sodom and Gomorrah (Genesis 19)
56. The New Jerusalem (Revelation 22:5)
57. Salem (Genesis 14:18)
58. Jericho (Luke 19:1)
59. Joppa (Acts 10:5-20)
60. Jerusalem.
61. Anathoth (Jeremiah 1:1)
62. Antipatris (Acts 23:31)
63. Jericho (Joshua 2)
64. Gilgal (1 Samuel 11:14-15)
65. Damascus (2 Kings 8:7)
66. Colossae (Colossians 4:9)

67. In what two cities did King Jeroboam erect his golden calves?

68. In what town did Saul massacre eighty-five priests?

69. What city was Esau's home base?

70. What city of Cyprus was a site of Paul's preaching?

71. What city was the home of Naboth, whose vineyard Ahab wanted?

72. What was King Saul's hometown?

73. What city was punished by Gideon for refusing to feed his hungry troops?

74. What prophet hailed from the town of Tekoa?

75. Where was Paul when he received his famous "Macedonian vision"?

76. What city was home to the man who gave Jesus a burial place?

77. What was the site of Moses' burial place?

78. Where were the bodies of Saul and Jonathan nailed to a wall?

79. Where were a number of men slain for looking into the ark of the covenant?

80. Where did Elisha strike Syrian soldiers with blindness?

81. What Philistine city worshiped the god Baal-zebub?

82. Where was the witch Saul consulted?

83. What city was home to the most-praised church mentioned in Revelation?

84. Where was Samuel buried?

85. Where did Peter cure Aeneas?

86. What was the site of the Israelites' great victory, led by Jonathan, over the Philistines?

87. What was the place where Jacob and Laban parted company?

88. Where did Jesus raise a widow's son from the dead?

89. What Phoenician city was home to Hiram, who helped construct Solomon's temple?

90. In what Samaritan town did Jesus meet the woman at the well?

67. Dan and Bethel (1 Kings 12:29)
68. Nob (1 Samuel 22:18)
69. Petra (Genesis 36:1)
70. Salamis (Acts 13:4-5)
71. Jezreel (1 Kings 21:1-29)
72. Gibeah (1 Samuel 10:26)
73. Succoth (Judges 8:5-16)
74. Amos (1:1)
75. Troas (Acts 16:11)
76. Arimathea (Matthew 27:57-60)
77. Beth-peor (Deuteronomy 34:1-6)
78. Beth-shan (1 Samuel 31:8-13)
79. Beth-shemesh (1 Samuel 6:19-21)
80. Dothan (2 Kings 6:13)
81. Ekron (2 Kings 1:2)
82. Endor (1 Samuel 28:7-14)
83. Philadelphia (Revelation 3:7-13)
84. Ramah (1 Samuel 25:1)
85. Lydda (Acts 9:32-35)
86. Michmash (1 Samuel 14:1-23)
87. Mizpah (Genesis 31:49)
88. Nain (Luke 7:11-18)
89. Tyre (1 Kings 5:1-11)
90. Sychar (John 4:7)

91. What city was home to the tabernacle after the Israelites conquered Canaan?
92. What Phoenician city was home to evil Jezebel?

✦Palatial Living

1. Whose palace had a hand that wrote on the wall?
2. What king of Tyre sent materials for David's palace?
3. Who burned the royal palace of Israel with himself inside?
4. What Babylonian went insane while walking on the roof of his palace?
5. Who took thirteen years to build his palace?
6. What nation's ambassadors were taken on a tour of the palace by King Hezekiah?
7. Who had a coveted vineyard close to Israel's royal palace?
8. Who referred to the future Jerusalem temple as a "palace for the Lord God"?
9. Who served as a cupbearer in Persia's royal palace?
10. What king was assassinated in his palace by Pekah?
11. Who had a palace with marble pillars and beds of gold and silver?

✦Up on the Roof

1. When Samson pulled the building down, how many people had been sitting on the rooftop?
2. Who had a vision of unclean animals while in prayed on a housetop?
3. In the days of Ezra, what did some of the Jews build on their rooftops?

91. Shiloh (Joshua 18:1)
92. Sidon (1 Kings 16:31-33)

✦Palatial Living (Answers)

1. Belshazzar's (Daniel 5:5)
2. Hiram (2 Samuel 5:11)
3. Zimri (1 Kings 16:15-18)
4. Nebuchadnezzar (Daniel 4:28-33)
5. Solomon (1 Kings 7:1-12)
6. Babylon's (2 Kings 20:16-18)
7. Naboth (1 Kings 21:1-19)
8. David (1 Chronicles 29:1, 19)
9. Nehemiah (1:1; 2:1)
10. Pekahiah (2 Kings 15:25)
11. Ahasuerus (Esther 1:5-6)

✦Up on the Roof (Answers)

1. About three thousand (Judges 16:27)
2. Peter (Acts 10:9-16)
3. Booths in commemoration of the Feast of Tabernacles (Nehemiah 8:14-16)

4. Who prophesied judgment on the people of Jerusalem because they burned incense to idols on their roofs?
5. Who hid two Israelite spies up on her rooftop among stalks of flax?
6. What king saw his nude neighbor on a rooftop?
7. Who had intercourse on a rooftop with all his father's concubines?
8. What was the ailment of the man who was let down through a roof in Capernaum so he could be healed by Jesus?
9. Who slept on Samuel's roof when he visited with him?

◆Collapsible Buildings

1. Who caused thousands of deaths by toppling the two main pillars in a large building?
2. In Jesus' parable about houses, who had a house that collapsed when the rains came?
3. Whose children perished when the house they were feasting in collapsed in a storm?
4. What judge tore down the tower of Penuel and slaughtered the people of the city?
5. What building, mentioned by Jesus, killed eighteen people when it collapsed?
6. According to Jesus, what building would be so thoroughly destroyed that there would not be one stone left on another?

4. Jeremiah (19:13)
5. Rahab (Joshua 2:6)
6. David (2 Samuel 11:2-4)
7. Absalom (2 Samuel 16:22)
8. He was paralyzed (Mark 2:3-4)
9. Saul (1 Samuel 25-26)

✦Collapsible Buildings (Answers)

1. Samson (Judges 16:23-30)
2. The foolish man (Matthew 7:26-27)
3. Job's (Job 1:18-19)
4. Gideon (Judges 8:17)
5. The tower of Siloam (Luke 13:4)
6. The temple (Mark 13:1-2)

◆Up Against the Wall

1. What perfectly square city is described as having walls made of jasper?
2. What prophet was trapped against a wall by an angel with a drawn sword?
3. Who escaped through the wall of Damascus by being let down in a basket?
4. Whose body was fastened to the wall of Beth-shan by the Philistines?
5. Who sacrificed his son on the city wall when the Moabites were losing the battle to Israel?
6. What city was famous for its fallen walls?
7. What prophet measured the wall of the temple district?
8. Who built the walls of Jerusalem?
9. What foreign invader tore down the walls of Jerusalem?
10. What rebel against David was beheaded, with his head thrown over the wall of Abel to Joab?
11. Who stuck his spear in the wall when it failed to strike its intended target, David?
12. What warrior, the victim of a king's scheming, was killed when shot by arrows from the wall of Rabbah?
13. In what besieged city did the king, walking on the city wall, meet a woman who told him she had eaten her son for dinner?
14. What wine steward sat down and wept when he learned the walls of Jerusalem had not been rebuilt?

◆Opening Windows

1. Who died after falling out of a window during Paul's sermon?
2. What prophet ordered a king to shoot arrows out of a window?

✦Up Against the Wall (Answers)

1. The New Jerusalem (Revelation 21:18)
2. Balaam (Numbers 22:24)
3. Paul (Acts 9:25)
4. Saul's (1 Samuel 31:10)
5. Mesha, king of Moab (2 Kings 3:27)
6. Jericho (Joshua 6:20)
7. Ezekiel (42:20)
8. Solomon (1 Kings 9:15)
9. Nebuchadnezzar (2 Kings 25:10)
10. Sheba (2 Samuel 20:22)
11. Saul (1 Samuel 19:10)
12. Uriah the Hittite (2 Samuel 11:24)
13. Samaria (2 Kings 6:26-29)
14. Nehemiah (1:3-4)

✦Opening Windows (Answers)

1. Eutychus (Acts 20:9)
2. Elisha (2 Kings 13:17)

3. What king looked out of his window and saw Isaac and Rebekah wooing?
4. What wicked queen was thrown out of a window by her servants?
5. Who knelt toward Jerusalem and prayed looking out of his eastern window in Babylon?
6. Who let birds fly out of his ship's window?
7. Who let spies escape through a window by using a rope?
8. Who looked out her window and was ashamed to see her husband dancing in the street?
9. In what city did Paul escape a plot by going through a window in the city wall?
10. According to Malachi, what windows would be opened for people that tithed?
11. Who looked out his window and saw a young man being enticed by a prostitute?
12. Whose wife helped him escape from Saul by letting him down through a window?

◆Wells, Cisterns, and Other Large Containers

1. Who had a miraculous well opened up for him after he worked up a thirst in battle?
2. What king dug wells in the desert?
3. What king ordered the construction of the Sea, the great basin in the temple court?
4. What exiled woman was approached by an angel at a well?
5. What army man was at the well of Sirah when he was summoned to his death by Joab's men?
6. Who escaped from Absalom's men by hiding in a well?
7. Who met his future wife at a well in Midian?

3. Abimelech (Genesis 26:8)
4. Jezebel (2 Kings 9:30, 32)
5. Daniel (6:10)
6. Noah (Genesis 8:6)
7. Rahab (Joshua 2:15-21)
8. Michal, wife of David (2 Samuel 6:16)
9. Damascus (2 Corinthians 11:33)
10. The windows of heaven (Malachi 3:10)
11. Solomon, or whoever wrote Proverbs (7:6-10)
12. David (1 Samuel 19:12)

✦Wells, Cisterns, and Other Large Containers (Answers)

1. Samson (Judges 15:18-20)
2. Uzziah (2 Chronicles 26:10)
3. Solomon (1 Kings 7:23)
4. Hagar (Genesis 16:7-14)
5. Abner (2 Samuel 3:26-27)
6. Ahimaaz and Jonathan (2 Samuel 17:17-21)
7. Moses (Exodus 2:15-21)

8. Who found a wife for Isaac at the well of Nahor?
9. Who longed for a drink from the well at Bethlehem?
10. What book contains laws telling owners of cisterns what to do if a person or animal accidentally falls in?
11. What prophet was imprisoned in a cistern?
12. Who met his future wife by a well when she came to water her sheep?
13. Where did God pare down Gideon's troops to three hundred men?
14. Who had servants who named their wells Esek, Sitnah, Rehoboth, and Beersheba?
15. What son of Jacob nearly perished in a cistern?
16. Who promised the citizens of Jerusalem that they could be free to drink from their own cisterns if they would surrender to Assyria?
17. In what country did Jesus talk with an immoral woman beside a well?
18. Who tried to take the well of Beersheba away from Abraham?

✦Gates, Doors, and Other Openings

1. Who did God speak to about the "gates of death"?
2. What gate of Jerusalem was rebuilt under Nehemiah's leadership?
3. What faithful soldier, home on furlough, chose to sleep in front of the king' palace door instead of going home to his wife?
4. Who removed the massive doors from the gate of Gaza and carried them to a hill at Hebron?
5. According to what Moses told the Israelites, where were the words of God to be written?
6. Who shut up the door of Noah's ark?

8. Abraham's servant (Genesis 24)
9. David (2 Samuel 23:14-17)
10. Exodus (21:33-34)
11. Jeremiah (38:6)
12. Jacob (Genesis 29:1-12)
13. The well of Harod (Judges 7:1-7)
14. Isaac (Genesis 26:17-33)
15. Joseph (Genesis 37:22)
16. Rabshakeh (2 Kings 18:31)
17. Samaria (John 4:5-15)
18. Abimelech (Genesis 21:22-32)

✦Gates, Door, and Other Openings (Answers)

1. Job (38:17)
2. The Sheep Gate (Nehemiah 3:1)
3. Uriah, the husband of Bathsheba (2 Samuel 11:9)
4. Samson (Judges 16:3)
5. On the doorposts of their houses and on their gates
   (Deuteronomy 11:20)
6. God (Genesis 7:16)

7. What king removed the gold from the doors of the temple and gave it to the king of Assyria?
8. When Lot's two angelic visitors blinded the lecherous men of Sodom, what were the men scrambling to do?
9. At the first Passover, what were the Israelites told to apply to their doorposts?
10. According to Psalm 24, what is to be lifted up so that the king of glory may enter in?
11. Who rolled back the stone from Jesus' tomb?
12. According to Revelation, which of the seven churches in Asia did the Lord say that he had set before it an open door that no man could shut?
13. Who healed a lame man at the temple's Beautiful Gate?
14. In John's vision of the New Jerusalem, how many gates does the city have, and what are they made of?

✦Portable Places to Dwell

1. Who accepted an invitation to hide in a tent, and was then murdered by the woman who invited him?
2. What famous ship captain lived in a tent?
3. What, in the dream of a Midianite soldier, tumbled into the Midianite camp and flattened a tent?
4. Who took spoils from the fallen Jericho and buried them inside his tent?
5. Who took his wife to his mother's tent on their wedding night?
6. Who was "the father of such as dwell in tents"?
7. Who stored Goliath's armor in his tent?
8. What was the tent that was made according to God's specifications?
9. Who plundered the tents of the Syrians after the army fled their camp?

7. Hezekiah (2 Kings 18:16)
8. Finding the door to Lot's home (Genesis 19:11)
9. Lamb's blood (Exodus 12:7)
10. The gates and the everlasting doors (Psalm 24:7-9)
11. The angel of the Lord (Matthew 28:2)
12. Philadelphia (Revelation 3:8)
13. Peter and John (Acts 3:2-7)
14. Twelve, made of pearl (Revelation 21)

✦Portable Places to Dwell (Answers)

1. Sisera (Judges 4:17-21)
2. Noah (Genesis 9:21)
3. A cake of barley (Judges 7:13-14)
4. Achan (Joshua 7:21)
5. Isaac (Genesis 24:67)
6. Jabal (Genesis 4:20)
7. David (1 Samuel 17:54)
8. The tabernacle (Exodus 26:1-4)
9. The Samaritans (2 Kings 7:3-16)

10. Who commanded his descendants to always live in tents?

11. Who pitched a tent in Jerusalem to house the ark of the covenant?

12. Who killed an Israelite man and a Moabite woman inside the man's tent?

13. Who lived in tents in the wilderness of Sin?

14. Who did Noah say would dwell in the tents of Shem?

15. What rebel against David said, "Every man to his tents, O Israel"?

16. What prophet said, "The Lord shall save the tents of Judah"?

17. What king were the people of Israel rebelling against when they said, "To your tents, O Israel"?

18. Who compares her dark skin to the blackness of the "tents of Kedar"?

19. What prophet saw "the tents of Cushan in affliction"?

10. Jonadab (Jeremiah 35:6-10)
11. David (1 Chronicles 15:1)
12. Phinehas, Aaron's grandson (Numbers 25:6-8)
13. The Israelites (Exodus 33:10)
14. Japheth (Genesis 9:27)
15. Sheba (2 Samuel 20:1)
16. Zechariah (12:7)
17. Rehoboam (2 Kings 12:16)
18. The woman in the Song of Solomon (1:5)
19. Habakkuk (3:7)

PART 4
The Domestic Scene

✦So Many Children

1. What judge had 70 sons?
2. Who is the first child mentioned in the Bible?
3. Who was Noah's youngest son?
4. What king was the youngest of eight brothers?
5. Who was Joseph's younger son?
6. Who is the youngest son of Adam mentioned by name?
7. Who were the first twins mentioned in the Bible?
8. Which disciple was probably a twin?
9. Who died giving birth to Benjamin?
10. Was the prodigal son the older or younger son?
11. What wicked king of Israel had 70 sons?
12. Who had 19 sons and 1 daughter by his legitimate wives?
13. Who was older, Moses or Aaron?
14. Who was Jacob's youngest son?
15. Who was born first, Jacob or Esau?
16. What king of Judah had 28 sons and 60 daughters?
17. What court prophet of David's had 14 sons and 3 daughters?
18. What prophet spoke of a time of peace when a little child would lead the wild beasts?
19. Who made sacrifices in case any of his children had sinned?
20. Which epistle advises, "Children, obey your parents in the Lord"?
21. According to Malachi, who will come to turn the hearts of the children to their fathers?
22. What little-known judge of Israel had 30 sons?

✦So Many Children (Answers)

1. Gideon (Judges 8:30)
2. Cain (Genesis 4:1)
3. Ham (Genesis 9:18-24)
4. David (1 Samuel 17:12-14)
5. Ephraim (Genesis 41:51-52)
6. Seth (Genesis 4:25)
7. Jacob and Esau (Genesis 25:23-26)
8. Thomas (John 11:16)
9. Rachel (Genesis 35:16-18)
10. The younger (Luke 15:11-32)
11. Ahab (2 Kings 10:1)
12. David (1 Chronicles 3:1-9)
13. Aaron (Exodus 7:7)
14. Benjamin (Genesis 35:16-18)
15. Esau (Genesis 25:25-26)
16. Rehoboam (2 Chronicles 11:21)
17. Heman (1 Chronicles 25:5)
18. Isaiah (11:6)
19. Job (1:5)
20. Ephesians (6:1)
21. Elijah (Malachi 4:6)
22. Jair (Judges 10:3-4)

23. Who did Paul advise that a bishop must be able to control his own children?

24. In which gospel did Jesus predict that children rebelling against their parents would be a sign of the end times?

25. Which of the Ten Commandments states that children will be punished for their parents' sins?

26. Which gospel does not mention the little children coming to Jesus?

27. Who advised young Christians to stop thinking like children?

28. Which gospel says that the child Jesus grew up strong?

29. What prophet advised people to tell their children about the locust plague?

30. Which epistle advises fathers not to exasperate their children?

31. What book says that a child raised up in the right way will never depart from it?

32. What priest was too indulgent toward his spoiled sons?

33. What prophet had dishonest sons who took bribes?

34. Which son was Isaac partial to?

35. What king grieved and wailed over his wayward son?

36. Who was Jacob's favorite son?

37. Who made a little coat for her son every year when she went to offer the annual sacrifice?

38. Which psalm says that children are like arrows in the hands of a warrior?

39. What book mentions how wonderful grandchildren are?

40. What prophet named his sons Maher-shalal-hash-baz and Shear-jashub?

41. According to the Law, what is the penalty for anyone who attacks his mother or father?

42. What prophet talks about children dishonoring their parents, so that a man's enemies are in his own household?

23. Timothy (1 Timothy 3:4)
24. Mark (13:12)
25. The second (against graven images) (Exodus 20:4)
26. John
27. Paul (1 Corinthians 14:20)
28. Luke (1:80)
29. Joel (1:3)
30. Ephesians (6:4)
31. Proverbs (22:6)
32. Eli (1 Samuel 3:13)
33. Samuel (1 Samuel 8:3)
34. Esau (Genesis 25:28)
35. David (2 Samuel 18:33)
36. Joseph (Genesis 37:3)
37. Hannah (1 Samuel 2:19)
38. 127:4
39. Proverbs (17:6)
40. Isaiah (7:3; 8:1-4)
41. Death (Exodus 21:15)
42. Micah (7:6)

43. According to Deuteronomy, what must be done to a rebellious son who will not submit to discipline?

44. What judge of Israel had 40 sons and 30 grandsons?

45. What Old Testament man almost sacrificed his beloved son?

46. What judge of Israel sacrificed his daughter?

47. Who did Paul say had known the Scriptures from his infancy?

48. Which of Gideon's 70 sons (the youngest) was the only one to escape the plot of his scheming brother Abimelech?

49. Who were Perez and Zerah?

50. Who died after giving birth to a son named Ichabod?

51. Who said that we must change and become like children?

52. Which book says that children will not be put to death for their parents' sins?

53. Who told believers that the promises of God were for their children as well as themselves?

54. Which epistle says that parents are to provide for their children, not vice versa?

55. What prophet said, "Great shall be the peace of thy children"?

56. What prophet said that the son would not share the guilt of the father?

57. What prophet said he was neither a prophet nor a prophet's son?

58. Who envisioned a time when sons and daughters would prophesy?

59. Who asked his childless wife if he was not worth more to her than ten sons?

60. Who was told that she had a daughter-in-law who treated her better than seven sons could?

61. What king made a wise decision about a child claimed by two prostitutes?

62. Who was adopted by Mordecai as his own daughter?

63. What psalm advises dashing the babies of Babylon against stones?

43. He must be stoned (Deuteronomy 21:18-21)
44. Abdon (Judges 12:13-14)
45. Abraham (Genesis 22)
46. Jephthah (Judges 11:30-40)
47. Timothy (2 Timothy 3:15)
48. Jotham (Judges 9:1-5)
49. Twin sons of Judah and Tamar (Genesis 38:29-30)
50. The wife of Phinehas (1 Samuel 4:19-22)
51. Jesus (Matthew 18:3)
52. Deuteronomy (24:16)
53. Peter (Acts 2:39)
54. 2 Corinthians (12:14)
55. Isaiah (54:13)
56. Ezekiel (18:20)
57. Amos (7:14)
58. Joel (2:28)
59. Elkanah (1 Samuel 1:8)
60. Naomi (Ruth 4:15)
61. Solomon (1 Kings 3:16-28)
62. Esther (2:7)
63. Psalm 137:8-9

✦Multiple Marriages

1. What king had 700 wives and 300 concubines?
2. Who was the first man in the Bible mentioned as having more than one wife?
3. Who married sisters Rachel and Leah?
4. Who fathered 70 sons by his many wives?
5. Whose father had two wives named Hannah and Peninnah?
6. What hairy man had three wives named Judith, Bashemath, and Mahalath?
7. What early king had two wives named Ahinoam and Rizpah?
8. What woman was married to two of Judah's sons?
9. What New Testament woman had had at least five husbands?
10. Who asked Jesus a ridiculous question about a woman who successively married seven brothers?
11. Who had Mahlon and Boaz for husbands?
12. What woman, given to Phaltiel by her father Saul, was later reclaimed by David?
13. What king of Judah had 14 wives?
14. What Persian king had wives named Vashti and Esther?
15. What son of Solomon had 18 wives and 60 concubines?
16. Whose wives included Abigail, Maacah, Haggith, and Eglah?
17. What patriarch took Keturah as his third wife?
18. Who had two wives, one of them named Zipporah?
19. What king, much influenced by his dominating wife, also had other wives?
20. What judge of Israel gave up his Philistine wife to his friend?

✦Multiple Marriages (Answers)

1. Solomon (1 Kings 11:3)
2. Lamech (Genesis 4:19)
3. Jacob (Genesis 29:15-25)
4. Gideon (Judges 8:30)
5. Samuel (1 Samuel 1:1-2)
6. Esau (Genesis 26:24; 28:9)
7. Saul (1 Samuel 14:50; 2 Samuel 3:7)
8. Tamar (Genesis 38:6-10)
9. The woman at the well (John 4:6-19)
10. The Sadducees (Mark 12:18-25)
11. Ruth (Ruth 4:10, 13)
12. Michal (2 Samuel 3:13-16)
13. Abijah (2 Chronicles 13:21)
14. Ahasuerus (Esther 1:10-12; 2:1-17)
15. Rehoboam (2 Chronicles 11:21)
16. David (2 Samuel 12:8)
17. Abraham (Genesis 16:3; 23:19; 25:1)
18. Moses (Exodus 18:2; Numbers 12:1)
19. Ahab (1 Kings 20:7)
20. Samson (Judges 14:20)

◆Widow Women

1. Who probably left more widows than anyone else?
2. What lying woman was a widow for only about three hours?
3. What book of the Old Testament is named for a famous widow who became an ancestress of David?
4. Who became a widow because of King David's lust?
5. What aged prophetess in Jerusalem was a widow?
6. Who posed to Jesus a foolish riddle about a woman who was a widow several times over?
7. What commendable deed was done by a poor widow Jesus saw in the temple?
8. Which church in Greece is mentioned by Paul as having widows in need of care?
9. Which of Paul's proteges had widows under his jurisdiction?
10. What woman of Joppa gave away clothing to the widows?
11. What city was home to the widow whose son Jesus raised from the dead?
12. What parable of Jesus has a widow as the main character?
13. What infamous widow was thrown from a window after she had put on make-up?
14. What prophet revived the son of the widow of Zarephath?
15. What widow had a husband whom the Lord killed and, later, had an affair with her father-in-law?
16. What widow, the daughter-in-law of the priest Eli, had a baby named Ichabod?
17. What king was almost fooled by the conniving woman of Tekoa who pretended to be a poor widow?
18. Whose mother was a widow named Zeruah?
19. Which widows in Jerusalem were neglected in the daily distribution of funds?

✦Widow Women (Answers)

1. Solomon, since he had over seven hundred wives (1 Kings 11:3)
2. Sapphira, who conspired with her husband Ananias to lie to Peter about the property they had sold (Acts 5:5-10)
3. Ruth
4. Bathsheba (2 Samuel 11:26)
5. Anna (Luke 2:36-37)
6. The Sadducees (Mark 12:22)
7. She put two mites (coins) in the temple treasury (Mark 12:42)
8. The church at Corinth (1 Corinthians 7:8)
9. Timothy (1 Timothy 5:3)
10. Tabitha (Acts 9:39)
11. Nain (Luke 7:12-15)
12. The parable of the unjust judge (Luke 18:2-5)
13. Jezebel (2 Kings 9:30-37)
14. Elijah (1 Kings 17:8-24)
15. Tamar, wife of Er (Genesis 34:25)
16. The unnamed wife of Phinehas (1 Samuel 4:19)
17. David (2 Samuel 14:1-20)
18. King Jeroboam of Israel (1 Kings 11:26)
19. The Greek-speaking (Hellenic) Jews (Acts 6:1)

20. What king forced ten of his concubines to live as widows for the rest of their lives?

21. Who married King David after her drunken husband suffered a stroke and died?

22. Who suggested that Christian widows were better off not to remarry?

23. What prophet issued dire warning against people who took advantage of widows?

24. Who did Jesus accuse of "devouring widows' houses"?

25. What New Testament epistle mentions kindness to widows as a mark of true religion?

26. What great city does Isaiah predict will become like a helpless widow?

◆Weddings, Dowries, and Divorces

1. Who made a wedding feast before giving the wrong bride to Jacob?

2. What gruesome objects did Saul require from David as dowry for his daughter?

3. Who prompted the Jews after the Babylonian exile to divorce their foreign wives?

4. Where was the first wedding Jesus attended?

5. Who, according to John, is the bride of Christ?

6. Who made a seven-day marriage feast but never married the woman?

7. Who gave the bride away at the first wedding?

8. How did Boaz obtain Ruth as his wife?

9. When Shechem the Hivite asked to marry Dinah, what did her brothers ask as a dowry?

10. What did Jacob have to do to marry Rachel?

11. Which gospel records Jesus' parable of a king's wedding feast for his son?

20. David (2 Samuel 20:3)
21. Abigail (1 Samuel 25:37-39)
22. Paul (1 Corinthians 7:8-9)
23. Malachi (3:5)
24. The Pharisees (Mark 12:40)
25. James (1:27)
26. Babylon (Isaiah 47:8)

✦Weddings, Dowries, and Divorces (Answers)

1. Laban (Genesis 29:22-25)
2. A hundred Philistine foreskins (1 Samuel 18:25, 27)
3. Ezra (Ezra 10)
4. Cana (John 2:1-11)
5. The church (Revelation 19:7-9)
6. Samson (Judges 14:10-20)
7. God (Genesis 2:22-24)
8. He purchased the property of Naomi, her mother-in-law (Ruth 3-4)
9. That all of Shechem's men be circumcised (Genesis 34:1-16)
10. Serve her father for fourteen years (Genesis 29:16-30)
11. Matthew (22:1-14)

12. Who sent the servant woman Hagar away at his wife's urging?

13. What unscrupulous king divorced his first wife to marry his brother's wife?

14. In Jesus' parable, how many virgins were to accompany the bride and groom?

15. Who arranged Ishmael's marriage?

16. Who was the first polygamist?

17. Who said that Moses allowed divorce because of people's hardness of heart?

18. Where does the Bible prohibit polygamy?

19. What prophet spoke about Jews divorcing their wives to marry pagan woman?

20. What was the levirate law?

21. What was considered proof of the bride's virginity?

22. Which gospel states that Jesus considered adultery to be grounds for divorce?

23. According to Jeremiah, who did God divorce?

24. What morally upright man wanted to quietly break off his engagement?

25. Which of Elkanah's wives was his favorite?

26. Who was thrown into prison for criticizing the marriage of a king?

27. Which of Paul's epistles gives the most information about marriage?

28. What Egyptian woman did Joseph marry?

29. Who was Naomi's husband?

30. What wife of David was also married to Nabal?

31. What king of Judah married a daughter of Ahab?

32. What Persian emperor married a Jewish girl?

33. What godly priest had a wife named Jehosheba?

34. Who married a prostitute named Gomer?

35. Who was married to Zebedee, father of James and John?

36. What childless woman was married to the priest Zacharias?

37. What wicked Persian official had a wife named Zeresh?

12. Abraham (Genesis 21:9-14)
13. Herod (Matthew 14:3-4)
14. Ten (Matthew 25:1-13)
15. Hagar, his mother (Genesis 21:21)
16. Lamech (Genesis 4:19)
17. Jesus (Matthew 19:8)
18. It doesn't.
19. Malachi (2:10-16)
20. When a man died without children, his brother was expected to take his wife so as to provide descendants for the dead man (Genesis 38:8-10)
21. A blood-stained cloth (Deuteronomy 22:13-21)
22. Matthew (19:3-12)
23. Israel (Jeremiah 3:8)
24. Joseph (Matthew 1:19)
25. Hannah (1 Samuel 1:1-8)
26. John the Baptist (Matthew 14:3-4)
27. 1 Corinthians (7)
28. Asenath (Genesis 41:45)
29. Elimelech (Ruth 1:2)
30. Abigail (1 Samuel 25:3)
31. Joram, who married Athaliah (2 Kings 8:21, 26)
32. Ahasuerus (Esther 2:16)
33. Jehoiada (2 Chronicles 22:11)
34. Hosea (1)
35. Salome (Matthew 4:21; Mark 16:1)
36. Elisabeth (Luke 1:5)
37. Haman (Esther 5:14; 6:13)

38. What saintly woman was the wife of Cuza, the head of Herod's household?
39. What Jewish-Christian couple were probably Paul's closest married friends?
40. What husband and wife lied to Peter about their finances?
41. What Roman governor had a Jewish wife named Drusilla?
42. Who took a wife that was not only nameless but ancestor-less?
43. What unknown wife turned into a pillar of salt?
44. What judge had a Philistine wife?
45. What unnamed wife urged her husband to curse God?
46. What leprous Syrian soldier had a faithful wife?
47. What prophet was married to a prophet?
48. What prophet had a wife who died suddenly?
49. What wicked priest had a harlot wife?
50. Whose wife insisted that her husband have nothing to do with Jesus?
51. Who was Moses' first wife?
52. Who was the only disciple that we know for sure was married?

✦Miraculous Pregnancies

1. Who gave birth to a son when she was 90 years old?
2. What beloved wife of Jacob gave birth after many years to Joseph and Benjamin?
3. What elderly couple produced a child, in accordance with the words of an angel?
4. Who prophesied to the Shunammite woman that, though her husband was too old, she would bear a child?
5. Why did God cause barrenness among the women of Abimelech's household?

38. Joanna (Luke 8:3)
39. Aquila and Priscilla (Acts 18:2)
40. Ananias and Sapphira (Acts 5)
41. Felix (Acts 24:24)
42. Cain (Genesis 4:17)
43. Lot's wife (Genesis 19:26)
44. Samson (Judges 14)
45. Job's wife (Job 2:9-10)
46. Naaman (2 Kings 5:1-4)
47. Isaiah, whose wife was called a prophetess (Isaiah 8:3)
48. Ezekiel (24:18)
49. Amaziah (Amos 7:10-17)
50. Pilate's (Matthew 27:19)
51. Zipporah (Exodus 2:21)
52. Peter (Mark 1:30)

◆Miraculous Pregnancies (Answers)

1. Sarah (Genesis 21:1-5)
2. Rachel (Genesis 30:22-24; 35:18)
3. Elisabeth and Zacharias (Luke 1:7-9, 13, 18)
4. Elisha (2 Kings 4:13-17)
5. Abimelech had taken Sarah for himself (Genesis 20:17-18)

6. What woman, long barren, gave birth to twins?
7. Who was taunted by her husband's other wife for being childless, though she later bore a son?
8. Whose astounded mother called herself the "handmaiden of the Lord" when told she would bear a child?
9. Whose mother was told by an angel that she would bear a son who would deliver Israel from the Philistines?
10. What very old man remarried after his wife's deaths and continued to father children?

✦Brother Against Brother

1. Whose older brother refused to attend the welcome home party?
2. What son of Gideon killed seventy of his brothers at once?
3. What judge, an illegitimate son, was thrown out of the house by his brothers?
4. Who hated his brother for taking away his birthright?
5. What did Moses rebuke Aaron for?
6. Who was the first man to murder his brother?
7. Who hated his brother Ammon for what he had done to Tamar?
8. What dreamy boy was hated for being his father's favorite?
9. What older brother of David chewed him out for coming to watch the Israelites fighting the Philistines?

6. Rebekah (Genesis 25:21-26)
7. Hannah, mother of Samuel (1 Samuel 1:1-19)
8. Jesus' (Luke 1:26-38)
9. Samson's (Judges 13:3, 5)
10. Abraham (Genesis 25:1-6)

✦Brother Against Brother (Answers)

1. The prodigal son's (Luke 15:28)
2. Abimelech (Judges 9:1-5)
3. Jephthah (Judges 11:1-2)
4. Esau (Genesis 27:41)
5. Making the golden calf (Exodus 32:19-22)
6. Cain (Genesis 4:8)
7. Absalom (2 Samuel 13:22)
8. Joseph (Genesis 37:4)
9. Eliab (1 Samuel 17:28-30)

✦Speaking of Beds

1. Who had a huge bed made of iron?
2. What king sulked in bed because he couldn't acquire a certain piece of property?
3. What church was threatened with being thrown on a "bed of suffering"?
4. Whose bedridden mother-in-law was healed by Jesus?
5. What son of a king was murdered and decapitated while lying asleep in bed?
6. Who blessed the twelve tribes while lying in bed?
7. What book of the Old Testament speaks fondly of a "verdant bed"?
8. What prophet condemned the idle rich on their beds of ivory?
9. What bedridden palsied man was healed by Peter?
10. What was Jesus trying to prove when he told the lame man to take up his bed and walk?
11. According to Hebrews, what bed should be kept pure?
12. What scheming son of a king took to his bed in order to take advantage of his sister?
13. What king of Judah was murdered in his bed by his servants?
14. Who raised a dead boy by laying him on a bed and lying on top of him?
15. Who saved her husband's life by putting an idol in his bed, covering it, and pretending it was him?
16. Who tried to coax Joseph into going to bed?
17. What king of Israel was told by Elijah that he would never get up from the bed he was lying on?
18. Who put a bed in her home for the prophet Elisha?

◆Speaking of Beds (Answers)

1. Og, king of Bashan (Deuteronomy 3:11)
2. Ahab (1 Kings 21:4)
3. The church of Thyatira (Revelation 2:22)
4. Peter's (Mark 1:30)
5. Ishbosheth, son of Saul (2 Samuel 4:7)
6. Jacob (Genesis 47-49)
7. The Song of Solomon (1:16)
8. Amos (6:4)
9. Aeneas (Acts 9:33-34)
10. That the Son of man had authority to forgive sins (Matthew 9:1-8)
11. The marriage bed (Hebrews 13:4)
12. Amnon (2 Samuel 13:5)
13. Joash (2 Chronicles 24:25)
14. Elijah (1 Kings 17:19) and Elisha (2 Kings 4:34)
15. Michal, wife of David (1 Samuel 19:11-17)
16. Potiphar's wife (Genesis 39:7)
17. Ahaziah (2 Kings 1:4)
18. The rich woman of Shunem (2 Kings 4:10)

PART 5
Things to Eat and Drink

✦Food, Food, Food

1. Who was famous as an eater of locusts?
2. What four faithful young men refused to eat the rich foods of the king of Babylon?
3. Who traded his bread-and-lentil stew for his brother's birthright?
4. Who had a baker who made pastries for him?
5. What incident in David's life caused people to bring him all manner of foods to eat?
6. According to the Law, what was the Passover meal to be composed of?
7. What old man was deceived when his son dressed in goatskin gloves and presented him with a meal of cooked goat?
8. Who served cheese, milk, and veal to the Lord when he made his appearance in the form of three men?
9. What did Ezekiel's edible scroll taste like in his mouth?
10. What judge of Israel cooked an angel a meal that included a pot of broth?
11. In what book of the Bible is Canaan first described as a land flowing with milk and honey?
12. What prized animal was killed for food when the prodigal son returned home?
13. In what country did the Hebrews feed on cucumbers, melons, leeks, onions, and garlic?
14. When Jacob's sons made a second trip to Egypt, what food did they bring with them as a gift for Joseph?

✦Food, Food, Food (Answers)

1. John the Baptist (Matthew 3:4)
2. Daniel, Shadrach, Meshach, and Abednego (Daniel 1:3-16)
3. Jacob (Genesis 25:29-34)
4. The pharaoh of Joseph's time (Genesis 40:16-17)
5. His flight from the rebellious Absalom (2 Samuel 17:22-29)
6. A cooked lamb, unleavened bread, and bitter herbs (Exodus 12:3-10)
7. Isaac (Genesis 27:14-18)
8. Abraham (Genesis 18:1-8)
9. Honey (Ezekiel 3:3)
10. Gideon (Judges 6:19)
11. Exodus (3:8)
12. The fatted calf (Luke 15:23)
13. Egypt (Numbers 11:5)
14. Almonds (Genesis 43:11)

15. What prophet, who was a herdsman and fruit picker by trade, had a vision of a basket of ripe fruit?
16. Who ate honey out of a lion's carcass?
17. What miraculous food resembled coriander seed?
18. What prophet purified some deadly stew and a water supply?
19. Who cursed a fig tree for not bearing fruit?
20. What ominous winged creature is described as unclean in the Law?

◆Sweet, Sour, Bitter, Poison

1. Who ate a book that tasted like honey?
2. According to Jeremiah, what kind of grape sets the children's teeth on edge?
3. What kind of herbs were the Israelites supposed to eat with the Passover meal?
4. Who posed a riddle about finding something sweet in a lion's carcass?
5. According to Jesus after the Resurrection, what would his followers be able to drink?
6. What substance—probably very bitter—did Moses make the people of Israel drink?
7. Who ate a book that was sweet at first but turned bitter afterwards?
8. According to Proverbs, what kind of water is sweet?
9. What sweet substance was part of John the Baptist's diet?
10. What prophet made some poison stew edible by pouring meal into it?
11. According to Proverbs, what kind of bread is sweet to a man?
12. What did Moses do to make the bitter waters of Marah drinkable?
13. Who told the repentant people of Israel to go home and enjoy sweet drinks?

15. Amos (8:1)
16. Samson (Judges 14:5-9)
17. Manna (Exodus 16:31)
18. Elisha (2 Kings 2:19-22; 4:38-41)
19. Jesus (Matthew 21:14)
20. The bat (Leviticus 11:13-19)

✦Sweet, Sour, Bitter, Poison (Answers)

1. Ezekiel (2:9-3:3)
2. Sour (Jeremiah 31:29)
3. Bitter herbs (Exodus 12:8)
4. Samson (Judges 14:14)
5. Poison (Mark 16:17-18)
6. Gold dust from the golden calf Moses had destroyed (Exodus 32:20)
7. John (Revelation 10:9-10)
8. Stolen water (Proverbs 9:17)
9. Honey (Matthew 3:4)
10. Elisha (2 Kings 4:41)
11. Bread of deceit (Proverbs 20:17)
12. Threw a piece of wood into the water (Exodus 15:25)
13. Nehemiah and Ezra (Nehemiah 8:10)

14. In Revelation, what falls on the earth's waters to make them bitter?
15. According to Proverbs, what sort of person thinks even bitter things are sweet?

◆Starvation Dieting

1. Which of the four horsemen in Revelation spreads famine on the earth?
2. Who moved with Naomi to Moab to escape famine?
3. Who was food storage supervisor in Egypt when famine came?
4. What nation was the victim of a seven-year famine during Elisha's ministry?
5. Where did Abram go when famine struck?
6. What New Testament prophet predicted a worldwide famine?
7. Who went to live with the Philistines during a famine?
8. What two plagues probably caused famine in Egypt?
9. What king's reign saw a three-year famine, which ended when Elijah said rain was coming?
10. What figure in a parable found himself the victim of famine?
11. What king endured famine because Saul had slain the Gibeonites?
12. In the time of the judges, what marauders plundered so many crops and livestock that they probably caused famine in Israel?
13. What Babylonian king caused famine in Jerusalem?
14. Who sent his sons to Egypt because of famine in the land?

14. A star (Revelation 8:10)
15. A hungry person (Proverbs 27:7)

✦Starvation Dieting (Answers)

1. The rider on the black horse (Revelation 6:5-6)
2. Elimelech (Ruth 1:1-2)
3. Joseph (Genesis 41)
4. Israel (2 Kings 8:1-2)
5. Egypt (Genesis 12:10)
6. Agabus (Acts 11:28)
7. Isaac (Genesis 26:1)
8. Locusts and hail (Exodus 10:14-15)
9. Ahab's (1 Kings 17:1; 18:44-45)
10. The prodigal son (Luke 15:14)
11. David (2 Samuel 21:1)
12. The Midianites (Judges 6:3-6)
13. Nebuchadnezzar (2 Kings 25:1-3)
14. Jacob (Genesis 42:1-2)

✦Banquets and Feasts

1. What king had a feast where a mysterious hand wrote on the wall?
2. Who threw a royal feast where his wife disobeyed him?
3. Who spread a meal for some angels at the oaks of Mamre?
4. Who gave a wedding feast and then pulled a trick on his son-in-law?
5. Whose children were killed while attending a feast?
6. Who told a bizarre riddle at his wedding feast?
7. What Pharisee had a feast that Jesus attended?
8. In Revelation, what holy figure has a wedding feast?
9. Where did Jesus have a post-Resurrection fish dinner with seven of his disciples?
10. What dweller in Sodom had a meal prepared for angelic visitors?
11. What Egyptian official had a feast prepared for his kinsmen from back home?
12. What ruler threw a lavish feast where his wife's daughter danced?
13. At the last feast mentioned in the Bible, what is to be the gruesome food?
14. In what village did Jesus have his first dinner after his Resurrection?
15. What child was given a feast on the day he was weaned?
16. What city had a wedding feast where Jesus' first miracle was done?
17. What prophet served his team of oxen at his ordination feast?
18. What tax collector had a feast for Jesus?
19. What army man was given a feast when he joined the side of David?
20. Who gave a feast for the evil Haman?
21. Who was given a three-day feast when he began to reign over all Israel?

✦Banquets and Feasts (Answers)

1. Belshazzar (Daniel 5)
2. Ahasuerus (Esther 1:3-12)
3. Abraham (Genesis 18:1-8)
4. Laban (Genesis 29:22-23)
5. Job's (Job 1:13)
6. Samson (Judges 14:10-14)
7. Simon (Luke 7:36-50)
8. The Lamb (Revelation 19:9)
9. By Lake Tiberias (John 21:1-13)
10. Lot (Genesis 19:3)
11. Joseph (Genesis 43:16-34)
12. Herod (Mark 6:21)
13. The flesh of people and horses (Revelation 19:17-18)
14. Emmaus (Luke 24:30)
15. Isaac (Genesis 21:8)
16. Cana (John 2:1-12)
17. Elisha (1 Kings 19:21)
18. Levi (Luke 5:29)
19. Abner (2 Samuel 3:20)
20. Esther (7:1-10)
21. David (1 Chronicles 12:39)

22. Who held a long feast when the Jerusalem temple was dedicated?
23. In the parable of the wedding feast, what is the fate of the man who did not put his best clothes on?
24. What town was the scene of the feast where Jesus was anointed with expensive perfume?
25. Who was given a banquet by King Ahasuerus when his beauty contest was over?
26. Who was given a feast where the entree was a fatted calf?
27. Who gave his officials a feast after God had spoken to him in a dream?

◆Fasts and Breaking of Fasts

1. What did Jesus eat after his Resurrection to prove he was not a mere phantom?
2. Who fasted for forty days on Mount Sinai?
3. Who had a Passover meal with his followers in the upper room?
4. Who received meals at the hands of birds?
5. Who was raped after bringing a meal to her supposedly sick brother?
6. What meat was eaten at the Passover meal?
7. Who sold his birthright for a bowl of soup?
8. Who humbled himself and fasted when accused of Naboth's murder?
9. Who fasted after his child by Bathsheba died?
10. How many men had bound themselves by an oath to fast until they had killed Paul?
11. Who prepared a meal for two angels in Sodom?
12. Who obtained his father's blessing by preparing him a meal and pretending to be his brother?
13. What was the first sinful meal?
14. Who fasted for forty days after his baptism?

22. Solomon (1 Kings 8:65)
23. He is tied up and thrown outside (Matthew 22:1-13)
24. Bethany (John 12:1-8)
25. Esther (2:17-18)
26. The prodigal son (Luke 15:23)
27. Solomon (1 Kings 3:15)

✦Fasts and Breaking of Fasts (Answers)

1. Fish (Luke 24:38-43)
2. Moses (Exodus 34:27-28)
3. Jesus (Matthew 26:1-30)
4. Elijah, fed by ravens (1 Kings 17:3-6)
5. Tamar (2 Samuel 13:1-14)
6. Lamb (Exodus 12:1-20)
7. Esau (Genesis 25:29-34)
8. Ahab (1 Kings 21:27)
9. David (2 Samuel 12:15-16)
10. Forty (Acts 23:20-21)
11. Lot (Genesis 19:1-3)
12. Jacob (Genesis 27:1-29)
13. The forbidden fruit (Genesis 3:6)
14. Jesus (Matthew 4:1-2)

15. Who was on a ship with 275 passengers who fasted for fourteen days?

16. What Roman official was fasting and praying when an angel told him to send for Peter?

17. Who read the prophecy of Jeremiah when the people of Jerusalem gathered for a fast?

18. What prophet's preaching drove the people of Nineveh to fast?

19. Who fasted before leaving Babylonia for Jerusalem?

20. Who angered his father by unwittingly breaking a fast while pursuing the Philistines?

21. What two apostles prayed and fasted as they chose elders for the churches?

22. What king of Judah proclaimed a fast when the Moabites attacked?

23. What pagan king fasted after Daniel had been thrown into the lions' den?

24. Who proclaimed a day of fasting as part of the scheme to get Naboth's vineyard?

25. What, according to Jesus, do prayer and fasting accomplish?

26. Who was Paul waiting for while he fasted three days in Damascus?

27. What king fasted all day and night while unsuccessfully inquiring of the Lord?

28. What official in the Persian court fasted before presenting his case to the king?

29. Who fasted and wore sackcloth as he prayed for the liberation of his people from Persia?

30. What church's elders fasted before sending Paul and Barnabas out as missionaries?

31. Where were the Israelites when Samuel had them fasting because of their idolatry?

32. In what country were the Jews when they fasted after learning of an executive order to have them all killed?

15. Paul (Acts 27:33)
16. Cornelius (Acts 10:1-3)
17. Baruch (Jeremiah 36:9-10)
18. Jonah (3:4-10)
19. Ezra (8:21-23)
20. Jonathan (1 Samuel 14:24-27)
21. Paul and Barnabas (Acts 14:23)
22. Jehosphaphat (2 Chronicles 20:1-4)
23. Darius (Daniel 6:18)
24. Jezebel (1 Kings 21:8-10)
25. Driving out demons (Matthew 17:21)
26. Ananias (Acts 9:9)
27. Saul (1 Samuel 28:20)
28. Nehemiah (1:1-4)
29. Daniel (9:3-4)
30. Antioch's (Acts 13:1-3)
31. Mizpah (1 Samuel 7:3-6)
32. Persia (Esther 4:1-3, 15-16)

33. Whose death caused the people of Jabesh-Gilead to fast for seven days?
34. After Ezra had read the law to the people, what was the main sin that caused them to fast?

◆Fruit of the Vine

1. What did Paul recommend as a substitute for wine?
2. Who was called a glutton and a wine guzzler?
3. What prophet spoke of God putting Israel into a winepress?
4. What part of the body did Paul recommend wine for?
5. Where was the one place the priest could not enter after drinking wine?
6. What group of Israelites was never supposed to drink wine?
7. According to Paul's advice, what church official must not be a wine drinker?
8. What was mingled with the wine Jesus was offered on the cross?
9. What judge threshed wheat by his winepress to hide it from the Midianites?
10. According to Jesus, what do people prefer, old wine or new wine?
11. What kind of person, according to Proverbs, should be given wine?
12. According to what Jesus said at the Last Supper, when would he drink wine again with his disciples?
13. Who murdered the Midianite Zeeb at his winepress?
14. How many jars of water did Jesus turn into wine?
15. What, according to Jesus, happens when new wine is put into old wineskins?
16. What drinkers did Isaiah condemn?
17. According to Romans, what good reason is there to avoid wine?

33. Saul and Jonathan's (1 Samuel 31:13)
34. Marrying foreigners (Nehemiah 9:1-3)

✦Fruit of the Vine (Answers)

1. The Holy Spirit (Ephesians 5:18)
2. Jesus (Matthew 11:19)
3. Isaiah (63:1-4)
4. The stomach (1 Timothy 5:23)
5. The tabernacle (Leviticus 10:8-9)
6. The Nazarites (Numbers 6:2-3)
7. A bishop (or overseer) (1 Timothy 3:2-3)
8. Myrrh (Mark 15:23)
9. Gideon (JUdges 6:11)
10. Old wine (Luke 5:39)
11. The sad or afflicted person (Proverbs 31:6-7)
12. When the kingdom had come (Matthew 26:27-29)
13. Gideon's army (Judges 7:25)
14. Six (John 2:1-10)
15. The wineskins burst (Luke 5:37-38)
16. Those who start early in the morning (Isaiah 5:11)
17. It might cause a brother to stumble (Romans 14:21)

✦Under the Influence

1. What husband, the victim of David's adulterous scheming, was made drunk by the king?

2. What man was seduced by his daughters while he was drunk?

3. Who dropped dead as a stone on hearing bad news the morning after being drunk?

4. What virtuous man, who later married a virtuous woman, passed out in a heap of grain while intoxicated?

5. Absalom wanted to avenge the rape of his sister, Tamar, so he waited until the rapist was very drunk. Who was this drunk, later slain by Absalom's men?

6. This king of Israel, who ruled barely two years, was assassinated while drunk. Who was he?

7. What Syrian king was getting drunk at a time when he was supposed to be making war on the Samaritans?

8. Nehemiah waited until this Persian king was softened up with wine before he asked the king to let the Jews return to their homeland. Who was the king?

9. What Persian queen refused to obey her drunken husband's order that she appear before his besotted guests?

10. Job's sons and daughters were so busy eating and drinking that they failed to notice that disaster was about to strike. What killed them?

11. The arrogant Babylonian king Belshazzar, drunk at his feast committed an outrage when he asked for new drinking vessels to be brought in. What were these vessels that led to so much trouble for the king?

✦Under the Influence (Answers)

1. Uriah, the husband of Bathsheba (2 Samuel 11:13)
2. Lot (Genesis 19:30-36)
3. Nabal, Abigail's husband (1 Samuel 25:36-37)
4. Boaz, husband of Ruth (Ruth 3:7-14)
5. Amnon, Absalom's half-brother (2 Samuel 13:28)
6. Elah (1 Kings 16:9)
7. Ben-hadad (1 Kings 20:12-19)
8. Artaxerxes (Nehemiah 2:1)
9. Vashti (Esther 1:3-12)
10. A great wind storm (Job 1:13-18)
11. Vessels from the temple of Jerusalem (Daniel 5:1-5)

PART 6
Matters of
Life and
Death

◆Strange Ways to Die

1. Who is the first individual who is killed by God for being wicked?
2. What devoured Aaron's sons, Nadab and Abihu, when they offered "strange fire" to the Lord?
3. What Canaanite captain was killed when Jael, a Hebrew woman, drove a tent peg through his skull?
4. Who was killed for touching the ark of the covenant?
5. The Lord sent a pestilence on Israel that killed 70,000 people. What act of King David brought this on?
6. God sent fire from heaven to kill the soldiers who came to capture what prophet?
7. What husband and wife dropped dead after it was revealed they had lied about the price of the possessions they had sold?
8. Who was hanged on the very gallows he had prepared for Mordecai?
9. What people were killed by great hailstones from heaven?
10. Who, along with his household, was swallowed up by the earth for rebelling against Moses?
11. What man, reluctant to produce children with his widowed sister-in-law, was slain by God?
12. What two cities were rained on by fire and brimstone?
13. What did God do when the Israelites began to complain about the death of Korah and his followers?

◆Strange Ways to Die (Answers)

1. Er (Genesis 38:7)
2. Fire from God (Leviticus 10:1-2)
3. Sisera (Judges 4:18-21)
4. Uzzah (2 Samuel 6:6-7)
5. He numbered the people of Israel (2 Samuel 24:1-5)
6. Elijah (2 Kings 1:10,12)
7. Ananias and Sapphira (Acts 5:1-10)
8. Haman (Esther 7:10—8:2)
9. Amorites (Joshua 10:8-14)
10. Korah (Numbers 16)
11. Onan (Genesis 38:9-10)
12. Sodom and Gomorrah (Genesis 19:24-25)
13. He sent a plague that killed 14,700 Israelites (Numbers 16:41-50)

14. What was the last plague sent upon the Egyptians?
15. What son of Saul was murdered by two servants who stabbed him in the belly and carried his severed head to David?

✦Back from the Dead

1. What prominent leader of Israel was summoned up from the dead by a witch?
2. Eutychus, who died after falling out of a window during a sermon, was raised from the dead by whom?
3. What prophet revived the son of the Zarephath widow?
4. Who raised Dorcas from the dead?
5. What man of Bethany was raised from his tomb by Jesus?
6. A man came to life again when his body came into contact with the buried bones of what prophet?
7. What was the name of the town where Jesus raised a widow's son from the dead?
8. Who did Elisha raise from the dead?
9. According to Matthew, what marvelous event occurred in conjunction with Jesus' death on the cross?
10. Whose daughter did Jesus bring back to life?

✦People Getting Stoned

1. Who pelted David and his men with stones while he accused David of being a violent man?
2. What son of a priest was stoned to death by order of King Joash?

14. The death of the firstborn (Exodus 12:29)
15. Ishbosheth, slain by Recab and Baanah (2 Samuel 4:5-8)

✦Back From The Dead (Answers)

1. Samuel (1 Samuel 28:7-20)
2. Paul (Acts 20:9-10)
3. Elijah (1 Kings 17:17-22)
4. Peter (Acts 9:36-41)
5. Lazarus (John 11:1-44)
6. Elisha (2 Kings 13:20-21)
7. Nain (Luke 7:11-15)
8. The son of the Shunammite woman (2 Kings 4:32-35)
9. Many holy people came out of their graves (Matthew 27:52-53)
10. Jairus' (Luke 8:41-42, 49-55)

✦People Getting Stoned (Answers)

1. Shimei (2 Samuel 16:5-6)
2. Zechariah (2 Chronicles 24:20-22)

3. What owner of a vineyard was stoned after being falsely accused in front of Ahab?

4. Who was stoned by an irate mob while trying to carry out the orders of King Rehoboam?

5. Which of Jesus' parables talks about the stoning of a landowner's servant?

6. Who was in danger of being stoned after the Amalekites dragged off the wives and children of Ziklag?

7. What shepherd boy felled a giant with a single stone?

8. Who stoned the Amorites while Joshua led an attack on them?

9. Who was stoned for holding back some of the loot from Jericho?

10. For what seemingly minor offense did the Israelites stone a man while in the wilderness?

11. In what city did some Jews persuade the people to stone Paul?

12. Who fled from Iconium when they heard of a plot to stone them?

13. What deacon became the first Christian martyr when the Jews stoned him?

14. What gospel mentions Jesus miraculously passing through a crowd that intended to stone him?

15. Who intended to stone the woman caught in adultery?

◆All of These Diseases

1. What afflicted the Philistines when they captured the ark of the covenant?

2. Where did Jesus encounter a woman who had had an unnatural flow of blood for many years?

3. What king of Judah suffered from a painful boil?

4. What apostle's mother-in-law had a fever?

3. Naboth (1 Kings 21:13)
4. Adoniram (1 Kings 12:18)
5. The parable of the tenants (Matthew 21:35)
6. David (1 Samuel 30:6)
7. David (1 Samuel 17:49)
8. The Lord (Joshua 10:11)
9. Achan and his family (Joshua 7:24-25)
10. Gathering sticks on the sabbath (Numbers 15:36)
11. Lystra (Acts 14:19)
12. Paul and Barnabas (Acts 14:5-6)
13. Stephen (Acts 7:59)
14. John (10:31, 39; 8:59)
15. The scribes and the Pharisees (John 8:3-11)

✦All of These Diseases (Answers)

1. Tumors (1 Samuel 5:6)
2. Capernaum (Matthew 9:20)
3. Hezekiah (2 Kings 20:7)
4. Peter's (Matthew 8:14-15)

5. What was the affliction of the government official's son healed by Jesus?
6. What righteous man suffered from boils?
7. According to Revelation, what afflicts those who have the mark of the beast?
8. What king of Judah suffered from a crippling foot disease?
9. In the parable of Lazarus and the rich man, what was Lazarus' affliction?
10. What son of Jonathan was crippled because he had been dropped by his nurse as a baby?
11. What man was healed of dysentery by Paul?
12. Who healed Aeneas of paralysis?
13. What was the affliction of the man let down through a roof by his friends?
14. What prophet said that all of Israel was covered with sores, wounds, and bruises?
15. What did Moses toss in the air to produce boils on the Egyptians?

✦A Time to Weep

1. Who wept at thinking her son would die of thirst in the desert?
2. Who wept over the death of his rebellious son, Absalom?
3. What Old Testament woman is pictured as "weeping for her children and refusing to be comforted"?
4. At whose death did Abraham weep?
5. Who wept at seeing the new temple that was built after the exiles' return from Babylon?
6. Whose second husband, Phaltiel, wept as he watched her return to her first husband, David?
7. What caused Nehemiah to weep?
8. Who cried as he begged Isaac for his rightful blessing?

5. Fever (John 4:52)
6. Job (2:7)
7. Painful sores (Revelation 16:2)
8. Asa (1 Kings 15:23)
9. Running sores (Luke 16:20)
10. Mephibosheth (2 Samuel 4:4)
11. Publius' father (Acts 28:8)
12. Peter (Acts 9:33)
13. Paralysis (Luke 5:18)
14. Isaiah (1:6)
15. Ashes (Exodus 9:9-10)

✦A Time to Weep (Answers)

1. Hagar, mother of Ishmael (Genesis 21:16)
2. David (2 Samuel 18:33)
3. Rachel (Jeremiah 31:15)
4. Sarah's (Genesis 23:2)
5. Old men who remembered the glory of Solomon's temple (Ezra 3:12)
6. Michal's (2 Samuel 3:16)
7. He heard the walls of Jerusalem were still in ruins (Nehemiah 1:4)
8. Esau (Genesis 27:38)

9. Who wept because her husband's other wife taunted her for being childless?
10. Who wept because he realized David had a chance to kill him but chose not to?
11. Who said, "Oh, that my head were waters, and mine eyes a fountain of tears"?
12. Who wept when he thought Joseph was dead?
13. Jacob wept with love and joy over what beautiful woman?
14. Who cried in Egypt when his brothers did not recognize him?
15. What judge's wife wept in front of him?
16. What three men wept when they saw Job's misery?
17. What prophet mentions women weeping for the god Tammuz?
18. What New Testament epistle mentions the priest Melchizedek weeping?
19. Who did Jesus tell not to weep for him?
20. What king's decree for extermination caused the Jews to weep?
21. Who said, "Mine eye poureth out tears to God"?
22. What king of Israel wept in front of the prophet Elisha?
23. What two male friends wept together?
24. When Saul was king, what caused the people of Gibeah to wail in despair?
25. What prophet cried when he realized what Hazael of Syria would do to the people of Israel?
26. What king of Judah cried because of his terrible illness?
27. Who wept with relief when he realized all his sons had not been killed?
28. The elders of what church wept over Paul?
29. Where was Paul when his friends wept at hearing the prophecy that Paul would be handed over to the Gentiles?
30. Who wept bitterly after denying Jesus?

9. Hannah (1 Samuel 1:7)
10. Saul (1 Samuel 24:16)
11. Jeremiah (9:1)
12. Jacob (Genesis 27:35)
13. Rachel (Genesis 29:11)
14. Joseph (Genesis 42:24)
15. Samson's (Judges 14:16)
16. Eliphaz, Bildad, and Zophar (Job 2:12)
17. Ezekiel (8:14)
18. Hebrews (5:6-7)
19. The daughters of Jerusalem (Luke 23:28)
20. Ahasuerus' (Esther 4:3)
21. Job (16:20)
22. Joash (2 Kings 13:14)
23. David and Jonathan (1 Samuel 20:41)
24. The threat of attack by the Ammonites (1 Samuel 11:4)
25. Elisha (2 Kings 8:11)
26. Hezekiah (2 Kings 20:3)
27. David (2 Samuel 13:36)
28. Ephesus (Acts 20:37)
29. Caesarea (Acts 21)
30. Peter (Matthew 26:75)

31. What baby was crying when he was discovered by a princess?
32. Who wept at her husband's feet and tried to dissuade him from listening to the advice of his assistant?
33. Who was reading the words of the Law when the people began to weep?
34. To whom did Jesus say, "Weep not"?
35. What friend did Jesus mourn for?
36. What king received approval from God for weeping and tearing his clothes in repentance?
37. Who wept and said to Jesus, "I believe; help thou my unbelief"?
38. Who wept on seeing what the Amalekites had done to the people of Ziklag?
39. Who discovered the widows of Joppa weeping over the dead Tabitha?
40. Where was Jesus when the sinful woman wiped his feet with her tears?

◆Sackcloth and Ashes

1. What rich man sat in a pile of ashes?
2. What pagan city wore sackcloth as a sign of repentance?
3. Who wore sackcloth when he heard Joseph had perished?
4. What prophet declared that the people of Jerusalem should put on sackcloth in view of the coming destroyer?
5. What prophet in Babylon wore sackcloth while seeking the Lord?
6. What prophet told the people to mourn in sackcloth like a young woman bewailing her lost husband?
7. What king was confronted by a prophet who had disguised himself with ashes?

31. Moses (Exodus 2:6)
32. Esther (8:3)
33. Ezra (Nehemiah 8:9)
34. The widow of Nain (Luke 7:13)
35. Lazarus (John 11:35)
36. Josiah (2 Chronicles 34:27)
37. The father of the boy with an evil spirit (Mark 9:24)
38. David (1 Samuel 30:4)
39. Peter (Acts 9:39)
40. The home of Simon the Pharisee (Luke 7:38)

◆Sackcloth and Ashes (Answers)

1. Job (2:8)
2. Nineveh (Jonah 3:8)
3. Jacob (Genesis 37:34)
4. Jeremiah (4:8)
5. Daniel (9:3)
6. Joel (1:8)
7. Ahab (1 Kings 20:37-39)

8. What book pictures the elders of Jerusalem sitting silently on the ground and wearing sackcloth?

9. What Syrian king had his servants wear sackcloth and grovel before King Ahab?

10. Who said, "I have sewed sackcloth upon my skin, and defiled my horn in the dust"?

11. What two cities did Jesus say would have repented in sackcloth and ashes if they could have seen his miracles?

12. Who put ashes on her head after being sexually assaulted by her lecherous half brother?

13. Who put on sackcloth when he learned of a government plan to wipe out the Jews?

14. Who was Job speaking to when he said, "I abhor myself, and repent in dust and ashes"?

✦Rending the Garments

1. What kinsmen of Joseph tore their clothes when they heard he had been killed?

2. What momentous finding caused King Josiah to tear his clothes?

3. Who tore his clothes when he heard his sons and daughters had all died at once?

4. Who tore his clothes when Jesus spoke of being seated at the right hand of God?

5. Who tore his clothes when he heard of the intermarriages of Jews with foreigners?

6. Whose oration caused King Hezekiah to tear his clothes?

7. Who tore their clothes on seeing Job's pitiful condition?

8. Who tore their clothes when Joseph's cup was found in Benjamin's sack?

9. Whose death caused David to order the people to tear their clothes?

8. Lamentations (2:10)
9. Ben-Hadad (1 Kings 20:31-32)
10. Job (16:15)
11. Tyre and Sidon (Matthew 11:21)
12. Tamar (2 Samuel 13:19)
13. Mordecai (Esther 4:1-3)
14. God (Job 42:6)

✦Rending the Garments (Answers)

1. Reuben his brother and Jacob his father (Genesis 37:29, 34)
2. The finding of the Book of the Law in the temple (2 Kings 22:11, 19)
3. Job (1:20)
4. The high priest (Matthew 26:65)
5. Ezra (9:3-5)
6. The Assyrian Rabshakeh's (2 Kings 19:1)
7. His three friends (Job 2;12)
8. Joseph's brothers (Genesis 44:13)
9. Abner's (2 Samuel 3:31)

10. What queen tore her clothes when she was put out of power by Jehoiada the priest?
11. Who tore their clothes when the people of Lystra began to worship them as gods?
12. What judge tore his clothing when his hasty words came back to haunt him?
13. What two men tore their clothes when the Israelites murmured against the Lord about going into Canaan?
14. Who rent his clothes when he heard Absalom had taken revenge on Amnon?
15. What man's assassination caused eighty men to come to Jerusalem with torn clothes and offerings of grain and incense?
16. What leper's plea for a cure caused the king of Israel to tear his clothes?
17. What warrior's death caused David and his men to tear their clothes in grief?
18. What friend of David, loyal during Absalom's rebellion, met David with torn robe and ashes on his head?
19. Who tore his clothes when Elijah was taken to heaven?
20. What abused sister tore her clothes after being raped by Amnon?

✦Grave Matters

1. What beheaded prophet was buried by his disciples?
2. What prophet's buried bones worked a miracle?
3. Who is the only person in the Old Testament mentioned as being buried in a coffin?
4. Who was buried in the cave of Machpelah?
5. What is the first burial of a servant mentioned in the Bible?
6. Who buried Moses?

10. Athaliah (2 Kings 11:14)
11. Paul and Barnabas (Acts 14:14)
12. Jephthah (Judges 11:35)
13. Joshua and Caleb (Numbers 14:6)
14. David (2 Samuel 13:31)
15. Gedaliah's (Jeremiah 41:4-5)
16. Naaman the Syrian's (2 Kings 5:7)
17. Saul's (2 Samuel 1:11)
18. Hushai the Archite (2 Samuel 15:32)
19. Elisha (2 Kings 2:12)
20. Tamar (2 Samuel 13:19)

✦Grave Matters (Answers)

1. John the Baptist (Matthew 14:11-12)
2. Elisha's (2 Kings 13:20-21)
3. Joseph (Genesis 50:26)
4. Abraham, Sarah, Isaac, Rebekah, Jacob, and Leah (Genesis 49:30-31; 50:13)
5. Deborah, Rebekah's nurse (Genesis 35:8)
6. The Lord (Deuteronomy 34:6)

7. What prophet, after being mourned by all Israel, was buried at Ramah?
8. What rebel was buried by Joab in a great pit in the forest?
9. What king's bones were, after his body was burned, buried at Jabesh-Gilead?
10. What was placed over Achan's body after the Israelites stoned him?
11. What leader was buried "in the border of his inheritance in Timnath-serah"?
12. Who was buried with Manoah, his father?
13. What judge died at a ripe old age and was buried in the grave of Joash, his father?
14. What evil king of Judah was buried, like his father, in the garden of Uzza?
15. What wicked king, the son of a godly king, was buried in the garden of Uzza?
16. Where were Joseph's bones finally buried?
17. What king was buried by his servants in the sepulchre with his forefathers in Jerusalem?
18. What leper king was buried in a special field?
19. What did the chief priests buy with the silver Judas returned to them?
20. What did Jesus say to the man who wanted time to bury his father?
21. Who begged the Canaanites for a place to bury his dead?
22. Who begged his son to be buried somewhere else besides Egypt?
23. What book says, "Their blood have they shed like water round about Jerusalem; and there was none to bury them"?
24. Who said, "The grave is my house"?
25. What book says that in the grave there is no work, no knowledge, and no wisdom?
26. Who said, "The grave cannot praise thee, death cannot celebrate thee"?
27. What apostle said, "O grave, where is thy victory?"

7. Samuel (1 Samuel 25:1)
8. Absalom (2 Samuel 18:17)
9. Saul's (1 Samuel 31:12-13)
10. Heaps of stones (Joshua 8:29)
11. Joshua (24:30)
12. Samson (Judges 16:31)
13. Gideon (Judges 8:32)
14. Amon (2 Kings 21:26)
15. Manasseh (2 Kings 21:18)
16. At Shechem (Joshua 24:32)
17. Ahaziah (2 Kings 9:28)
18. Uzziah (2 Chronicles 26:23)
19. A field to bury strangers in (Matthew 27:6-7)
20. "Let the dead bury their dead" (Matthew 8:22)
21. Abraham (Genesis 23:4)
22. Jacob (Genesis 47:29)
23. Psalms (79:3)
24. Job (17:13)
25. Ecclesiastes (9:10)
26. Hezekiah (Isaiah 38:18)
27. Paul (1 Corinthians 15:55)

28. What prophet, speaking the words of the Lord, said, "I will ransom them from the power of the grave"?

29. What figure is portrayed in these words by Isaiah: "He made his grave with the wicked, and with the rich in his death"?

30. To whom did the Israelites say, "Because there were no graves in Egypt, hast thou taken us away to die in the wilderness?"?

31. What gospel records the graves opening after Jesus' death on the cross?

32. Who said, "The hour is coming, in which all that are in the graves shall hear his voice"?

33. What people did Jesus refer to as "graves which appear not"?

34. According to Psalm 5, what is like an open sepulchre?

35. According to Jesus, the Pharisees built tombs for who?

36. Who gave his rock-cut tomb as a burial place for Jesus?

37. Who infuriated Isaiah by building an elaborate tomb for himself?

38. What man who hanged himself was buried in his family tomb?

39. Whose burial at Hebron caused the grief of David?

40. According to the Law, when was a hanged man's body supposed to be buried?

41. What wicked queen did Jehu send his men to bury, though she had already been devoured by dogs?

42. Who erected a memorial pillar for himself during his own lifetime?

43. What king had his body cast at the city gate with stones heaped on it?

44. What two liars were buried by the early Christians?

45. According to Jeremiah, what king was destined to have the burial of a donkey?

46. What woman, according to Jesus, prepared him for burial?

28. Hosea (13:14)
29. The Suffering Servant (Isaiah 53:9)
30. Moses (Exodus 14:11)
31. Matthew (27:52-53)
32. Jesus (John 5:28)
33. The scribes and the Pharisees (Luke 11:44)
34. The enemies' mouths (Psalm 5:9)
35. The prophets (Matthew 23:29)
36. Joseph of Arimathea (Luke 23:50-53)
37. Shebna (Isaiah 22:15-16)
38. Ahitophel (2 Samuel 17:23)
39. Abner's (2 Samuel 3:31)
40. The same day as the hanging (Deuteronomy 21:23)
41. Jezebel (2 Kings 9:34-37)
42. Absalom (2 Samuel 18:18)
43. The king of Ai (Joshua 8:29)
44. Ananias and Sapphira (Acts 5:6, 10)
45. Jehoiakim (Jeremiah 22:19)
46. The woman with the ointment (Matthew 26:12)

47. Who brought myrrh and aloes for the burial of Jesus?
48. According to Revelation, whose bodies would lie in the streets for three and half days without burial?
49. What two epistles compare baptism with burial?
50. Who buried Stephen?
51. Who did God promise would be buried at a ripe old age?
52. Who buried Abraham?
53. According to Jeremiah, who would not be buried or mourned?
54. What priest did Jeremiah tell he would be buried in Babylon?
55. Who buried Isaac?
56. What prophetess died and was buried at Kadesh?
57. What priest died and was buried at Mosera?
58. What judge of Israel was buried at Shamir?
59. What king was buried in Jerusalem after being killed by Pharaoh's armies?
60. What wicked king who had sacrificed his son was refused burial in the kings' sepulchres?
61. What king of Judah, murdered by his servants, was refused burial in the kings' sepulchres?
62. What judge of Israel was buried in Gilead?
63. Who moved the bones of Saul and Jonathan to their final burial place?
64. Who was the first king to be buried in Samaria?
65. What king was killed by Jehu and then cast into Naboth's field?
66. How long had Lazarus been in his tomb when Jesus came?
67. What king desecrated the tombs at Bethel, burning the bones on an altar?
68. What disturbed man lived among tombs?
69. What group of people told Abraham that they would not refuse him burial in their tombs?
70. In John's Gospel, who is the first person to see Jesus' empty tomb?

47. Nicodemus (John 19:39)
48. The two prophets (Revelation 11:3-9)
49. Romans (6:4) and Colossians (2:12)
50. Godly men (Acts 8:2)
51. Abraham (Genesis 15:15)
52. Isaac and Ishmael (Genesis 25:9)
53. The "slain of the Lord" (Jeremiah 25:33)
54. Pashur (Jeremiah 20:6)
55. Esau and Jacob (Genesis 35:29)
56. Miriam (Numbers 20:1)
57. Aaron (Deuteronomy 10:6)
58. Tola (Judges 10:1-2)
59. Josiah (2 Chronicles 35:24)
60. Ahaz (2 Chronicles 28:27)
61. Jehoash (2 Chronicles 24:25)
62. Jephthah (Judges 12:7)
63. David (2 Samuel 21:12-13)
64. Omri (1 Kings 16:28)
65. Jehoram (2 Kings 9:25)
66. Four days (John 11:17)
67. Josiah (2 Kings 23:16)
68. The Gerasene demoniac (Mark 5:2)
69. The Hittites (Genesis 23:5-6)
70. Mary Magdalene (John 20:1)

71. According to Matthew, who ordered the guard at Jesus' tomb?
72. What prophet referred to his unusual prison as a "grave"?
73. What prophet pictures the Lord preparing a grave for Nineveh?
74. What book compares the power of jealousy to the power of the grave?
75. What book says that the grave is one of the four things that can never be satisfied?
76. Who is the only person in the Bible pictured as wearing his grave clothes?
77. What wife of Jacob had a pillar erected upon her grave?
78. In the New Testament, what young man was raised from the dead while on his way to be buried?
79. What prophet heard God describing the armies of the heathen nations gathered around their own graves?
80. What prophet complained that his mother's womb should have been his grave?
81. In Luke's gospel, who is the only apostle to actually investigate the empty tomb?
82. In Matthew's gospel, who moved the stone from Jesus' tomb?

✦Death in Massive Doses

1. What nation saw 185,000 of its soldiers slaughtered by an angel of the Lord?
2. What judge and his men killed 120,000 Midianites?
3. When the Israelites lost 30,000 soldiers in the time of Samuel, who were they fighting?
4. What king headed up the slaying of 47,000 Syrians?
5. When the Jews were allowed to defend themselves against the Persians, how many Persians were killed?

71. Pilate (Matthew 27:65)
72. Jonah (2:2)
73. Nahum (1:14)
74. Song of Solomon (8:6)
75. Proverbs (30:16)
76. Lazarus (John 11:44)
77. Rachel (Genesis 35:19-20)
78. The son of the widow of Nain (Luke 7:14)
79. Ezekiel (32:17-31)
80. Jeremiah (20:17)
81. Peter (Luke 24:12)
82. An angel (Matthew 28:2)

◆Death in Massive Doses (Answers)

1. Assyria (2 Kings 19:35)
2. Gideon (Judges 8:10)
3. The Philistines (1 Samuel 4:10)
4. David (1 Chronicles 19:18)
5. 75,000 (Esther 9:15-16)

6. What king of Israel killed 20,000 men of Judah in one day because they had forsaken the Lord?

7. For what offense did the Lord kill 50,070 men of Beth Shemesh?

8. For what sin of David did the Lord kill 70,000 Israelites with a plague?

9. What king of Judah led an army that killed 500,000 soldiers of Israel?

10. What Syrian king fled when 100,000 of his soldiers were killed by the people of Israel?

◆Killed by the Beasts

1. What sinister creature came in droves and killed the people of Israel in the wilderness?

2. What son of Jacob was, according to his brothers, killed by a wild animal?

3. Which book mentions people being devoured by lions?

4. What prophet saw two female bears devour the children who had poked fun at his baldness?

5. What animals devoured the foreigners who had moved into Israel?

6. For what strange offense was a prophet killed by a lion?

7. What animal killed a man for disobeying the old prophet of Bethel?

6. Pekah (2 Chronicles 28:6)
7. For looking into the ark of the covenant (1 Samuel 6:19)
8. Taking a census (2 Samuel 24:15)
9. Abijah (2 Chronicles 13:17)
10. Ben-hadad (1 Kings 20:29)

◆Killed by the Beasts (Answers)

1. Fiery serpents (Numbers 21:6)
2. Joseph (Genesis 37:33)
3. Daniel (6:24)
4. Elisha (2 Kings 2:24)
5. Lions (2 Kings 17:24-25)
6. He refused the request of another prophet to hit him (1 Kings 20:35-36)
7. A lion (1 Kings 13:20-32)

PART 7
...And Things Left Over

✦Not to Be Taken Seriously (I)

1. What animal on the ark had the highest intelligence?
2. Which burns longer—a candle under a bushel or one on a hill?
3. What kind of lights did Noah use on the ark?
4. When was the rooster's crow heard by everyone on earth?
5. How many animals did Noah bring into the empty ark?
6. What are the two smallest insects in the Bible?
7. Why, according to the Bible, is it all right to be obese?
8. Who was the first canning factory run by?
9. What wage does not have any deductions?
10. Why couldn't they play cards on Noah's ark?
11. How are roller skates like the fruit in the Garden of Eden?
12. What day in human life was longest?
13. Why did the people on the ark think the horses were pessimistic?
14. What is often black, brown, or white, but should always be red?
15. What son of Noah was a real clown?
16. Which days in Bible times passed by quickly?
17. What was the most expensive meal in the Bible?
18. What was the Bible's first theatrical performance?
19. Where does the Bible talk about smoking?
20. When was tennis played in the Bible?
21. Why was building the tower of Babel such a sad project?
22. What came first—the chicken or the egg?

◆Not to Be Taken Seriously (I) (Answers)

1. The giraffe
2. Neither—both get shorter
3. Flood lights
4. When it crowed on the ark
5. One—after that it was not longer empty.
6. The widow's mite and the wicked flea. (See Mark 12:42 and Proverbs 28:1)
7. Because "all the fat is the Lord's" (Leviticus 3:16)
8. Noah—he had a boatful of preserved pairs.
9. The wages of sin
10. Because Noah sat on the deck
11. They come before the fall.
12. Adam's first day—it had no eve.
13. They were always saying neigh.
14. The Bible
15. Ham
16. Fast days
17. Esau's—it cost him his birthright
18. Eve's appearance for Adam's benefit
19. Genesis—Rebecca lighted off her camel
20. Joseph served in Pharaoh's court.
21. There were so many tiers.
22. The chicken—God doesn't lay any eggs.

✦Laughing and Dancing

1. What is the only book in the Bible to mention God laughing?
2. What epistle tells Christians to turn their laughter to mourning?
3. According to Psalm 126, what caused laughter among the Jews?
4. What book says there is a time to weep and a time to laugh?
5. What book says that laughter is foolishness?
6. What book says that even in laughter the heart is sorrowful?
7. What instrument is usually associated with dance in the Bible?
8. What book says, "Our dance is turned into mourning"?

✦Across the Biblical Spectrum

1. What color was the hideous seven-headed dragon in Revelation?
2. What is the first color mentioned in the Bible?
3. What doting father gave his favorite son a coat of many colors?
4. What New Testament woman was a seller of purple cloth?
5. What book describes a handsome man whose hair is black like a raven?
6. What prophet had a vision of four chariots pulled by different colored horses?
7. According to Isaiah, what color does the Lord wear?
8. According to Isaiah, what color are sins?
9. What color was the sun in Revelation when it became like sackcloth?
10. What fabulous animal is mentioned as churning up white foam in the sea?

✦Laughing and Dancing (Answers)

1. Psalms (2:4; 37:13; 59:8)
2. James (4:9)
3. Bringing the captives back to Jerusalem (Psalm 126:2)
4. Ecclesiastes (3:4)
5. Ecclesiastes (2:2)
6. Proverbs (14:13)
7. The timbrel, or tambourine (Exodus 15:20; Judges 11:34; Job 21:12; Psalm 150:4)
8. Lamentations (5:15)

✦Across the Biblical Spectrum (Answers)

1. Red (Revelation 12:3)
2. Green (Genesis 1:30—"I have given every green herb")
3. Jacob (Genesis 37:3)
4. Lydia (Acts 16:14)
5. Song of Solomon (5:11)
6. Zechariah (6:1-3)
7. Red (Isaiah 63:2)
8. Scarlet (Isaiah 1:18)
9. Black (Revelation 6:12)
10. Leviathan (Job 41:32)

11. Who, according to 2 Peter, had a place of deep blackness reserved for them?

12. What evil woman was dressed in purple and scarlet and covered with jewels?

13. According to Joel, what fateful day would be a day of blackness?

14. Which Old Testament book contains the most references to the color blue?

15. According to Psalms, what color is the sinner after being washed by God?

16. What color was the cloth draped over the ark of the covenant?

17. Who sang a victory song that mentions white donkeys?

18. What Gospel mentions Jesus commenting on the red sky as a weather omen?

19. In Mark's Gospel, what color was the robe Jesus wore when the soldiers mocked him?

20. What three colors was the curtain for the Holy of Holies in the temple?

21. What Jew wore the royal purple garments in a foreign court?

22. What prophet talked about idols dressed in blue and purple garments?

23. Who had a vision of a heavenly being with a white hair and white clothing?

24. What people defeated by Gideon wore purple garments?

25. What book speaks of an industrious wife who wears clothes of fine purple linen?

26. What prophet saw a drought end when the sky grew black?

27. What book mentions people who had worn purple pawing through the garbage of Jerusalem?

28. What servant of a prophet had his skin turned white as snow?

29. What colors were the fabrics used inside Solomon's temple?

11. False teachers (2 Peter 2:17)
12. Babylon, the great harlot (Revelation 17:4)
13. The day of the Lord (Joel 2:2)
14. Exodus (because of the many references to the tabernacle furnishings)
15. Whiter than snow (Psalm 51:7)
16. Blue (Numbers 4:6)
17. Deborah and Barak (Judges 5:10)
18. Matthew (16:2)
19. Purple (Mark 15:17)
20. Blue, red, and purple (2 Chronicles 3:14)
21. Mordecai (Esther 8:15) or Daniel (5:29)
22. Jeremiah (10:9)
23. Daniel (7:9)
24. The Midianites (Judges 8:26)
25. Proverbs (31:22)
26. Elijah (1 Kings 18:45)
27. Lamentations (4:5)
28. Gehazi, Elisha's servant (2 Kings 5:27)
29. Blue, red, and purple (2 Chronicles 2:14)

30. Which of Jesus' parables mentions a rich man dressed in purple robes?

31. What insect invasion made the Egyptian ground black?

32. Who prayed that the day he was born would be covered with blackness?

33. Who had a vision of horsemen with breastplates that were yellow like sulfur?

34. How many times does the Bible mention brown?

35. What book mentions an immoral woman covering her bed with colored sheets from Egypt?

36. What prophet saw a multicolored eagle carrying off the top of a cedar tree?

37. What disease was considered to be healed if healthy black hair was growing on the skin?

38. What creature eliminated every green thing from the land of Egypt?

39. In Revelation, what did the rider on the red horse bring to the earth?

40. What kind of pastures are mentioned in Psalm 23?

41. According to Proverbs, what kind of person thrives like a green leaf?

42. What prophet says that God is like a green tree giving shelter to those who trust him?

43. In Revelation, what caused the green grass on earth to be burned up?

44. What color do the armies of heaven, in Revelation, wear?

45. What color cord was the harlot Rahab supposed to tie to her window so the Israelites would recognize her home?

46. In Revelation, what did the rider on the black horse bring to the earth?

47. What book mentions a woman with lips like a scarlet ribbon?

48. What color was the horse in Revelation that carried a rider with a pair of scales in his hands?

30. The parable of the rich man and Lazarus (Luke 16:19)
31. Locusts (Exodus 10:15)
32. Job (3:5)
33. John (Revelation 9:17)
34. Once (the color of a horse) (Zechariah 1:8)
35. Proverbs (7:16)
36. Ezekiel (17:3)
37. Leprosy (Leviticus 11:31, 37)
38. The locusts (Exodus 10:15)
39. War (Revelation 6:4)
40. Green pastures.
41. A righteous person (Proverbs 11:28)
42. Hosea (14:8)
43. Hail, fire, and blood poured on the earth (Revelation 8:7)
44. White (Revelation 19:14)
45. Scarlet (Genesis 2:18)
46. Famine (Revelation 6:6)
47. Song of Solomon (4:3)
48. Black (Revelation 6:5)

49. According to Job, what animal searches for green things to eat in the mountains?

50. According to Matthew's Gospel, what color was the robe the Roman soldiers put on Christ when they mocked him?

51. What evil woman in Revelation rode on a scarlet beast?

52. In Revelation, what fallen city is noted as having dressed itself in scarlet and purple?

53. Where are black sheep mentioned in Bible?

54. Who practiced genetic engineering by using green and white branches in his flocks' drinking water?

55. What color were the clothes of the person who held seven stars in his hand?

56. What color hair was considered a symptom of leprosy?

57. What color was the cloth over the altar in the tabernacle?

58. What king promised purple robes for the man who could explain a strange inscription?

59. Who raised the question about whether there was flavor in the white of an egg?

60. Who, according to Lamentations, had their skin blackened after the fall of Jerusalem?

61. What book advises people always to wear white clothing?

62. According to Isaiah, what color would God change the scarlet sins to?

63. What prophet mentioned a harlot cavorting with soldiers in purple uniforms?

64. Who had a vision of ravenous locusts that devoured foliage and made the trees' branches white?

65. Where was Jesus when his clothes became radiantly white?

66. What color were the clothes of the angel that stood by Jesus' tomb?

67. What sweet food was white like coriander seed?

49. Wild donkeys (Job 39:8)
50. Scarlet (Matthew 27:28)
51. The great harlot (Revelation 17:3)
52. Babylon (Revelation 18:16)
53. Genesis 30:35—Laban had them in his flock.
54. Jacob (Genesis 30:37-42)
55. White (Revelation 1:14)
56. White (Leviticus 13:3)
57. Blue (Numbers 4:11)
58. Belshazzar (Daniel 5:7)
59. Job (6:6)
60. The princes (Lamentation 4:8)
61. Ecclesiastes (9:8)
62. White (Isaiah 1:18)
63. Ezekiel (23:6)
64. Joel (1:7)
65. The Mount of Transfiguration (Matthew 17:2)
66. White (Matthew 28:3)
67. Manna (Exodus 16:31)

68. What color stone was promised to the faithful people at the church of Pergamum?

69. What church was told to buy white clothes to cover its nakedness?

70. What color clothes were the twenty-four elders in Revelation wearing?

71. According to David, which leader had clothed the women of Israel in fine scarlet robes?

72. What color cow was to be burned so that its ashes could be used in removing uncleanness?

73. What color thread was tied around the arm of the firstborn of Tamar's twins?

74. Who complained that his skin had turned black?

75. What color were the pomegranates around the hem of the high priest's robes?

76. What people did Jesus compare to whitewashed tombs?

77. What person did Paul call a "whitewashed wall"?

78. Whose name means "red"?

79. What color were the cords on the tassels the Israelites were commanded to put on their garments?

80. What sea was parted by a wind from God?

81. In the Law, what color ram's skin was acceptable as an offering?

82. What color horse did Faithful and True ride?

83. According to Moses, what color is a grape's blood?

84. What people were frightened away when they mistook the redness of the morning sun on water for blood?

85. Whose face turned red with weeping?

86. What color was the first of the four horses in Revelation?

87. Who warned his followers that they could not change the color of their hair by worrying?

88. What color was the stew Esau begged Jacob to give him?

68. White (Revelation 2:17)
69. Laodicea (Revelation 3:18)
70. White (Revelation 4:4)
71. Saul (2 Samuel 1:24)
72. Red (Numbers 19:2)
73. Scarlet (Genesis 38:28)
74. Job (30:30)
75. Blue, red, and purple (Exodus 28:33)
76. The scribes and Pharisees (Matthew 23:27)
77. Ananias the high priest (Acts 23:3)
78. Edom (Esau's other name) (Genesis 25:30)
79. Blue (Numbers 15:38)
80. The Red Sea (Exodus 13:18)
81. Red (Exodus 25:5)
82. White (Revelation 19:11)
83. Red (Deuteronomy 32:14)
84. Moabites (2 Kings 3:22)
85. Job's (16:16)
86. White (Revelation 6:2)
87. Jesus (Matthew 5:36)
88. Red (Genesis 25:30)

89. According to Nahum, what city was attacked by soldiers in scarlet uniforms and carrying scarlet shields?

90. In Revelation, what did the rider on the white horse bring to the earth?

91. According to Proverbs, we should avoid looking at wine when it is what color?

92. What color horse did Death ride?

93. What color did the moon become when the sixth seal was broken open?

94. Which of Jacob's sons was described as having teeth whiter than milk?

95. What prophet mentions multicolored carpets?

96. Who had a throne with purple cushions?

97. What prophet said that prophets had whitewashed a pile of loose stones?

98. What Gospel says that the transfigured Jesus wore clothes whiter than anyone could every wash them?

99. What book mentions making robes white by washing them in blood?

100. What curious object was in the hand of the person sitting on the white cloud in Revelation?

◆Going to Extremes

1. Who was the youngest king mentioned in the Bible?
2. What was the largest army assembled?
3. What king of Judah had the longest reign?
4. What king of Israel had the shortest reign?
5. What is the shortest prayer in the Bible?
6. What are the two shortest verses in the Bible?
7. What is the longest verse in the Bible?
8. What is the longest prayer in the Bible?
9. What is the biggest animal mentioned in the Bible?
10. What is the smallest animal mentioned in the Bible?
11. What is the longest book in the Bible?

89. Nineveh (Nahum 2:3)
90. Conquest (Revelation 6:2)
91. Red (Proverbs 23:31)
92. Pale (or pale green, depending on your translation) (Revelation 6:8)
93. Blood red (Revelation 6:12)
94. Judah (Genesis 49:12)
95. Ezekiel (27:24)
96. Solomon (Song of Solomon 3:10)
97. Ezekiel (13:10)
98. Mark (9:3)
99. Revelation (7:14)—the blood of the Lamb makes them clean.
100. A sickle (Revelation 14:14)

NOTE: Answers may vary because the names of colors differ in different translations.

✦Going To Extremes (Answers)

1. Joash (or Jehoash), who began his reign at the age of seven (2 Chronicles 24:1)
2. One million men, brought by Zerah the Ethiopian against Asa of Judah (2 Chronicles 14:9)
3. Manasseh, who ruled for 55 years (2 Kings 21:1)
4. Zimri, who ruled for seven days after usurping the throne (1 Kings 16:15)
5. "Lord, save me," uttered by Peter while sinking (Matthew 14:30)
6. "Jesus wept" (John 11:35) and "Eber, Peleg, Reu" (1 Chronicles 1:25)
7. Esther 8:9—90 words in the King James Version
8. Probably Nehemiah's 9:5-38.
9. The whale (Genesis 1:21)
10. The gnat (Matthew 23:24)
11. Psalms

12. What is the longest book in the New Testament?
13. What word, the name of Isaiah's son, is the longest word in the Bible?
14. What is the longest chapter in the Bible?

◆Hairsbreadth Escapes

1. Paul, newly converted to Christianity, enraged the Jewish leaders in a certain city, so they decided to murder him. His friends let him down in a basket through the city wall. What city was it?

2. The judge Ehud stabbed the fat Moabite king Eglon while they were alone together. What simple maneuver did Ehud use to evade the king's guards?

3. Nebuchadnezzar breached the walls of Jerusalem, but the king and many others escaped. How?

4. The king of Sodom escaped his attackers by hiding where?

5. In Mark's Gospel, a young man who was following Jesus on the night of his betrayal just barely escaped from being apprehended himself. What was the sole garment the young man was wearing, and how did he escape?

6. Where did Joseph take Mary and the infant Jesus in order to escape the wrath of King Herod?

7. After Moses, still living in the royal household of Egypt, killed an Egyptian, where did he take refuge?

8. When a violent storm caused the death of all of Job's children, how many people in the household escaped the tragedy?

9. Jesus was threatened with stoning by people gathering in Jerusalem for the Feast of Dedication. How did he escape?

10. Of the many times Saul tried to kill David, one of the closest calls was when he threw a spear at David. What did David do?

12. Luke
13. Maher-shalal-hash-baz (Isaiah 8:1)
14. Psalm 119, with 176 verses

✦Hairsbreadth Escapes (Answers)

1. Damascus (Acts 9:19-25)
2. He locked the door to the king's chamber and escaped through an upstairs porch (Judges 3:25-26)
3. There was a secret gate next to the king's garden (2 Kings 25:1-5)
4. In slime pits (Genesis 14:9-11)
5. The garment was a linen cloth. When the men grabbed him by the cloth, he fled away naked (Mark 14:51-52)
6. To Egypt (Matthew 2:13)
7. In Midian (Exodus 2)
8. One (Job 1:14-19)
9. We don't know—the Gospel account gives no explanation (John 10:22-39)
10. He merely sidestepped the spear so it went into a wall (1 Samuel 19:10)

11. How did Michal, David's wife, fool the messengers who came to fetch the runaway David?
12. Running from Saul, David took refuge in Gath, where the king was worried at having a popular folk hero in town. How did David keep himself from being a victim of the king's anger?
13. When Absalom was trying to usurp the crown from his father, David, a woman helped David by hiding two of his messengers from Absalom's men. How did she hide them?

✦Hugs and Kisses

1. What two hostile brothers met and kissed each other, weeping all the way?
2. Who did Joab murder while kissing?
3. What prophet talked about kissing calves?
4. Who kissed Barzillai, an old man who had provided supplies for the army?
5. Who kissed Absalom after his two years in exile?
6. Who poured oil on Saul's head and kissed him?
7. What aged father kissed one son, mistaking him for the other?
8. Who met Moses in the wilderness and kissed him?
9. When Jacob died, who wept over him and kissed him?
10. What bereaved woman kissed her daughters-in-law goodbye as she left to return to her own country?
11. What rebel was so magnetic in personality that the men of Israel couldn't help kissing him?
12. Who kissed David when he was fleeing from Saul?
13. Who met Moses by the mount of God and kissed him?
14. Who kissed his brothers in a tearful family reunion?
15. Who kissed and blessed Ephraim and Manasseh, Joseph's sons?

11. She placed an idol (presumably human-sized) in David's bed and told the messengers he was sick (1 Samuel 19:11-18)
12. He pretended to be crazy (1 Samuel 21:10-15)
13. She hid them in a well, spread a covering over the well, and spread grain over the covering to hide it (2 Samuel 17:17-21)

✦Hugs and Kisses (Answers)

1. Jacob and Esau (Genesis 33:4)
2. Amasa (2 Samuel 20:9-10)
3. Hosea (13:2), who was referring to calf idols
4. David (2 Samuel 19:39)
5. David (2 Samuel 14:33)
6. Samuel (1 Samuel 10:1)
7. Isaac, who kissed Jacob instead of Esau (Genesis 27:27)
8. Jethro, his father-in-law (Exodus 18:5, 7)
9. Joseph (Genesis 50:1)
10. Naomi (Ruth 1:9)
11. Absalom (2 Samuel 15:5-6)
12. Jonathan (1 Samuel 20:41)
13. Aaron (Exodus 4:27)
14. Joseph (Genesis 45:15)
15. Jacob (Genesis 48:10, 20)

16. Who kissed his nephew the first time they met?
17. Who returned home after making peace with his son-in-law and kissing his grandchildren goodbye?
18. What book begins, "Let him kiss me with the kisses of his mouth: for thy love is better than wine"?
19. What book says, "Every man shall kiss his lips that giveth a right answer"?
20. Who had a tearful farewell, with many kisses, at the city of Miletus?
21. Which epistle says, "Greet with a kiss of charity"?
22. According to Proverbs, whose kisses are deceitful?
23. Where was Jesus when the sinful woman kissed his feet and anointed him?
24. Which epistles end with Paul's admonition to greet fellow Christians with a "holy kiss"?
25. Where is a kiss described as lustful?
26. Who kissed Jesus as a supposed sign of friendship?
27. Who kissed the prodigal son?
28. Which book says, "Kiss the Son, lest he be angry"?
29. Who kissed Rachel almost as soon as he met her?
30. What prophet protested men kissing the image of Baal?
31. To whom did Job speak about kissing the hand as an act of homage?

✦Foot Coverings

1. Who was told by God to take his shoes off because he was standing on holy ground?
2. Who told people that he was not worthy to carry the Messiah's sandals?
3. Who told a king that he would not accept a gift of shoelaces?
4. What book mentions the custom of giving a person one's shoe as a sign of transferring property?
5. What nation did God toss his shoes upon?

16. Laban, Jacob's uncle and future father-in-law (Genesis 29:13)
17. Laban (Genesis 31:55)
18. Song of Solomon (1:2)
19. Proverbs (24:26)
20. Paul (Acts 2:36-38)
21. 1 Peter (5:14)
22. An enemy's (Proverbs 27:6)
23. The home of Simon the Pharisee (Luke 7:36-43)
24. Romans (16:16), 1 Corinthians (16:20), 2 Corinthians (13:12), and 1 Thessalonians (5:26)
25. Proverbs 7:13
26. Judas (Matthew 26:48)
27. His father (Luke 15:20)
28. Psalms (2:12)
29. Jacob (Genesis 29:11)
30. Elijah (1 Kings 19:18)
31. Eliphaz, Bildad, and Zophar (Job 31:27)

✦Foot Coverings (Answers)

1. Moses (Exodus 3:5)
2. John the Baptist (Matthew 3:11)
3. Abram told this to the king of Sodom (Genesis 14:23)
4. Ruth (4:7)
5. Edom—"Over Edom will I cast out my shoe" (Psalm 60:8)

6. During what historic event were the Hebrews instructed to keep their shoes on and be ready to travel?

7. For what crime could a man have his shoe taken away and his face spit in?

8. What were the best-made shoes in the Bible?

9. Who did Jesus tell not to carry sandals with them on their journey?

10. What towns' people tricked Joshua by putting on worn-out shoes when they went to meet him?

11. What sea, according to Isaiah, would be dried up by the Lord so that men could walk over it in their shoes?

12. What prophet, once he had taken his shoes off, walked around barefoot for years?

13. According to Ezekiel, what city did God put leather sandals on?

14. Who was told not to take his shoes off after his wife died?

15. Which prophet accused the people of Israel of selling the poor people for a pair of sandals?

16. What book has a devoted lover praising a woman's sandaled feet?

17. Who was told by the commander of the heavenly army to take off his shoes?

18. Who ordered a pair of sandals for his son's feet?

19. Who was told by an angel to put on his clothes and shoes?

20. Who prophesied that soldiers' boots would be used as fuel for burning?

6. Passover (Exodus 12:11)
7. Refusing to marry the widow of his deceased brother (Deuteronomy 25:9)
8. The shoes of the Hebrews who left Egypt, since they lasted for forty years (Deuteronomy 29:5)
9. The disciples (Matthew 10:10)
10. The people of Gibeon (Joshua 9:5)
11. The Egyptian sea (Isaiah 11:15)
12. Isaiah (20:2)
13. Jerusalem (Ezekiel 16:10)
14. Ezekiel (24:17)
15. Amos (2:6)
16. Song of Solomon (7:1)
17. Joshua (5:15)
18. The father of prodigal son (Luke 15:22)
19. Peter (Acts 12:8)
20. Isaiah (9:5)

✦Stones, Rolling and Non-rolling

1. Who suggested that stones could be turned to bread?
2. Who used a stone for a pillow?
3. What enemies of Joshua were pelted by stones from the Lord?
4. In what humiliating way was Abimelech murdered?
5. Who had a vision of an angel casting an enormous stone into the sea?
6. Who erected a large pillar stone and called it Ebenezer?
7. What shepherd boy went into battle with a bag of stones?
8. Who built an altar of stone that was consumed by fire from heaven?
9. What patriarch and his father-in-law heaped up stones as a sign of their covenant together?
10. Who sat on a stone while the Amalekites fought the Israelites?
11. Who had a dream about a giant statue struck by a stone?
12. Which disciple was called a rock?
13. In Revelation, what did the Spirit promise to the churches that would overcome?
14. Who set up a commemorative stone after the Israelites covenanted to serve the Lord?
15. Which of Paul's epistles speaks about a "spiritual rock" that was Christ?
16. Who rolled the stone across the tomb when Jesus was buried?
17. Who spoke of a rejected stone becoming the chief cornerstone?
18. What friend of Jesus had a stone rolled over the front of his tomb?
19. Who rolled a stone from off a well so that Laban's flocks could be watered?

✦Stones, Rolling and Non-rolling (Answers)

1. Satan (Luke 4:3)
2. Jacob (Genesis 28:11-22)
3. The Amorites (Joshua 10:11)
4. A woman dropped a millstone on his head (Judges 9:53)
5. John (Revelation 2:17)
6. Samuel (1 Samuel 7:12)
7. David (1 Samuel 17:49)
8. Elijah (1 Kings 18:31-38)
9. Jacob and Laban (Genesis 31:44-52)
10. Moses (Exodus 17:8-12)
11. Nebuchadnezzar (Daniel 2:34-35)
12. Peter (Matthew 16:18)
13. A white stone (Revelation 2:17)
14. Joshua (24:27)
15. 1 Corinthians (10:4)
16. Joseph of Arimathea (Matthew 27:59-60)
17. Jesus (Matthew 21:42)
18. Lazarus (John 11:38-40)
19. Jacob (Genesis 29:10-11)

20. Who sealed up five Amorite chieftains in a cave by rolling large stones across the entrance?

21. Who was thrown into a den of wild animals that was sealed with a stone?

22. Who brought costly stones for the foundation of the temple in Jerusalem?

23. Who did Jesus tell that the stones would cry out if the people were silenced?

24. Who set up a commemorative pillar of stone at Paddan-Aram?

25. Who struck a rock and brought water from it?

26. Who prophesied that there would not be one stone of the temple that would not be thrown down?

27. Who picked up twelve souvenir stones from the dry path across the Jordan River?

28. Who had a garment with two onyx stones engraved with the names of the children of Israel?

29. Who wrote on tablets of stone for Moses?

30. Who had a breastplate with twelve precious stones in it?

31. What precious jewel is mentioned by Jesus in a parable about the kingdom?

32. What city is decorated with twelve precious stones?

33. What did Jesus say should not be cast before swine?

34. What did Job say was so precious it could not be purchased with gems?

35. What, according to Proverbs, is more precious than rubies?

36. What prophet said that Jerusalem would have walls made of jewels?

37. What city has gates made of pearl?

38. What epistle says that Christian women should not wear pearls?

39. What prophet talks about nine precious stones adorning the king of Tyre?

40. Which psalm says that the stone rejected by the builders becomes the chief stone?

---

20. Joshua (10:16-18)
21. Daniel (6:17)
22. Solomon (1 Kings 5:17)
23. The Pharisees (Luke 19:40)
24. Jacob (Genesis 35:9, 14)
25. Moses (Exodus 17:6)
26. Jesus (Mark 13:1-2)
27. Joshua (4:4-8)
28. Aaron (Exodus 28:9-12)
29. God (Exodus 24:12)
30. The high priest (Exodus 28:17-20)
31. The pearl (Matthew 13:45-46)
32. The New Jerusalem (Revelation 21:19-20)
33. Pearls (Matthew 7:6)
34. Wisdom (Job 28:16)
35. Wisdom (Proverbs 3:15)
36. Isaiah (54:12)
37. The New Jerusalem (Revelation 21:21)
38. 1 Timothy (2:9)
39. Ezekiel (28:11-13)
40. Psalm 118 (verse 22)

41. Who questioned Job about the cornerstone of the earth?
42. Who spoke about God laying a precious cornerstone for Jerusalem?
43. Which epistle refers to Christ as a living stone?
44. Which epistle says that the apostles and prophets are a foundation and Christ is the chief cornerstone?
45. Who was Peter addressing when he spoke of Jesus as the cornerstone?

✦Boats and Other Floating Things

1. What king's household was carried in the only ferry boat mentioned in the Bible?
2. What was the material used in making the basket the infant Moses was floating in?
3. Who joined with wicked King Ahaziah of Israel in building a navy to go to Tarshish?
4. What nervous prophet actually requested that he be thrown off a storm-tossed ship at sea?
5. What king of Israel had two navies?
6. What was Jesus doing when a storm struck the boat carrying him and his disciples?
7. What was the only ship in the Bible mentioned by name?
8. What was the name of the island where Paul and his companions landed after the shipwreck?
9. Who used a ship as a pulpit?
10. What two prophets predicted attacks from the war ships of Chittim?
11. What New Testament author uses the symbol of a ship's rudder to describe the power of the human tongue?

41. God (Job 38:6)
42. Isaiah (28:16)
43. 1 Peter (2:4-8)
44. Ephesians (2:20-22)
45. The Sanhedrin (Acts 4:11)

◆Boats And Other Floating Things (Answers)

1. David's (2 Samuel 19:16-18)
2. Bulrushes daubed with slime and pitch (Exodus 2:3)
3. King Jehoshaphat of Judah (2 Chronicles 20:35-57)
4. Jonah (1:4-16)
5. Solomon (1 Kings 9:26-28; 10:22)
6. Sleeping (Luke 8:22-24)
7. Castor and Pollux (Acts 28:11)
8. Malta (or Melita) (Acts 28:1)
9. Jesus (Luke 5:3)
10. Balaam (Number 24:24) and Daniel (11:30)
11. James (3:4)

12. Who sent timber, in the form of rafts, to King Solomon?
13. What prophet predicted a glorious day when God's people would not be threatened with attacking ships?
14. What was Noah's ark made of?

✦Them Bones, Them Bones

1. What weapon did Samson use to kill a thousand men?
2. Whose bones were buried under a tree at Jabesh?
3. Who was made from a single bone?
4. Who was spared having his bones broken because he had already died?
5. Who had a vision of a valley filled with men's dry bones?
6. What saintly king desecrated a pagan altar by burning human bones on it?
7. What prophet's bones had sufficient power to raise another man from the dead?
8. What leader, carefully buried in an Egyptian coffin, had his bones transported out during the exodus and was buried at Shechem?
9. Which psalm contains a lament that passersby can count the psalmist's bones?

✦Things in Baskets

1. What king received seventy human heads in baskets?
2. What apostle owed his life to a basket?
3. What ill-fated servant had a dream of three bread baskets?
4. How many basketful of food were collected after the feeding of the five thousand?

12. Hiram of Tyre (1 Kings 5:8-9)
13. Isaiah (33:21)
14. Gopherwood (Genesis 6:13-16)

✦Them Bones, Them Bones (Answers)

1. The jawbone of an ass (Judges 15:15)
2. Saul's and his sons' (1 Samuel 31:11-13)
3. Eve (Genesis 2:21-22)
4. Jesus (John 19:33, 36)
5. Ezekiel (37:1-14)
6. Josiah (2 Kings 23:16)
7. Elisha's (2 Kings 13:20-21)
8. Joseph (Joshua 24:32)
9. Psalm 22 (verse 17)

✦Things in Baskets (Answers)

1. Jehu (2 Kings 10:7)
2. Paul (Acts 9:25)
3. Pharaoh's baker (Genesis 40:16-17)
4. Twelve (Matthew 14:20)

5. Who had a vision of two baskets of figs in front of the temple?
6. What prophet had a vision of a basket of summer fruits?
7. Who had a vision of a wicked woman rising up out of a basket?
8. What future liberator was found floating in a basket in the river?
9. Who served an angel a young goat in a basket?
10. How many basketsful of food were collected after the feeding of the four thousand?

◆As a Reminder

1. What was given as a reminder that the world would never again be destroyed by a flood?
2. What ritual was to be a reminder of Christ's body and blood?
3. What day of the week is a reminder of God's completed creation?
4. What was the manna put into the ark of the covenant a reminder of?
5. What festival was to be a memorial of the Jews' salvation from the wicked Persian Haman?
6. What feast was to be a reminder of the simple homes the Israelites had in Egypt?
7. What feast was a reminder of the death angel killing the Egyptian firstborn?
8. Who made brazen lights to remind the people of Israel that no one except Aaron's descendants should serve as priests?
9. What woman did Jesus say would have her story remembered for doing a kindness to him?
10. Who set up twelve stones to remind the people of God's power in bringing them across the Jordan?

5. Jeremiah (24:1)
6. Amos (8:1)
7. Zechariah (5:7)
8. Moses (Exodus 2:3-5)
9. Gideon (Judges 6:19)
10. Seven (Matthew 15:37)

✦As a Reminder (Answers)

1. The rainbow (Genesis 9:13-16)
2. The Lord's Supper (Luke 22:19)
3. The Sabbath (Deuteronomy 5:15)
4. God's supernatural provision in the desert (Exodus 16:32)
5. Purim (Esther 9:28)
6. The Feast of Tabernacles (Leviticus 23:39-43)
7. Passover (Exodus 12:11-14)
8. Eleazar (Numbers 16:39-40)
9. The woman who anointed his feet at Bethany (Matthew 26:6-13)
10. Joshua (4:7)

✦A Sign Unto You

1. What was given as a sign that the shepherds had found the baby Jesus?
2. What was given as a sign that God would not flood the earth again?
3. What gift was given to Christians as a sign of God's power to unbelievers?
4. What day was a sign of completion and rest?
5. According to Jesus, what prophet's sign would be given to the unbelieving Jews?
6. Who received a wet fleece as a sign of God's approval?
7. Who prophesied a virgin conceiving a child as a sign of God's presence?
8. Who saw a "slow" sundial as a sign of Hezekiah's recovery from illness?
9. Who set up twelve stones as a sign of God's parting of the Jordan?
10. What nation suffered ten plagues that were signs of God's power?
11. What food was a sign of the deliverance from Egypt?
12. What king saw an altar broken as a sign that God was speaking through a prophet?
13. What prophet advised building a signal fire as a sign of the coming invasion of Babylon?

✦Lamps, Candles, Etc.

1. Who had a vision of Jesus walking among seven gold candlesticks?
2. Who told a story about ten women lighting their lamps to meet a bridegroom?
3. Who saw a torch from God pass between the animals he had brought to sacrifice?
4. Which psalm says, "Thy word is a lamp unto my feet, and a light unto my path"?

✦A Sign Unto You (Answers)

1. The swaddling clothes and the manger (Luke 2:12)
2. A rainbow (Genesis 9:13-17)
3. Tongues (1 Corinthians 14:22)
4. The Sabbath (Exodus 31:13)
5. Jonah's (Matthew 16:4)
6. Gideon (Judges 6:36-38)
7. Isaiah (7:14)
8. Isaiah (2 Kings 20:8-11)
9. Joshua (4:6)
10. Egypt (Exodus 10:2)
11. Unleavened bread (Exodus 13:7-9)
12. Jeroboam (1 Kings 13:5)
13. Jeremiah (6:1)

✦Lamps, Candles, Etc. (Answers)

1. John (Revelation 1:12)
2. Jesus (Matthew 25:1)
3. Abraham (Genesis 15:17)
4. Psalm 119 (verse 105)

5. Who was told to make a seven-branched candlestick to place inside the tabernacle?
6. According to Jesus, where do we never put our light?
7. What king sang, "For thou art my lamp, O Lord, and the Lord will lighten darkness"?
8. What man, seeing his headquarters collapse, called for a light to check on Paul and Silas?
9. What judge confused the Midianite army by having his men break the jars they were using as lanterns?
10. According to the New Testament, what city has no need of lamps or candles?
11. In Jesus' parable, what was the woman who searched her house with a lantern looking for?

◆Threads and Ropes and Chains

1. What hyperactive person broke all the chains that had been used to bind him?
2. Who dropped a scarlet cord from her window to aid the Israelite spies?
3. Who made chains strung with pomegranates to decorate the temple?
4. Who put a chain of gold around Daniel's neck?
5. What people had golden chains around their camels' necks?
6. What apostle had his chains removed by an angel?
7. Who bound King Zedekiah in chains and blinded him?
8. Who gave birth to twins, one of which had a scarlet thread tied around it by the midwife?
9. Who put a golden chain around Joseph's neck?
10. What judge was bound up in cords by the Philistines?
11. What prophet was bound up in chains, along with the others who were carried away as captives?

5. Moses (Exodus 25:31-37)
6. Under a bushel (Matthew 5:15)
7. David (2 Samuel 22:29)
8. The Philippian jailor (Acts 16:29)
9. Gideon (Judges 7:16-21)
10. The New Jerusalem (Revelation 22:5)
11. A lost coin (Luke 15:8)

✦Threads and Ropes and Chains (Answers)

1. The Gadarene demoniac (Mark 5:3-4)
2. Rahab the harlot (Joshua 2:15-19)
3. Solomon (2 Chronicles 3:16)
4. Belshazzar (Daniel 5:29)
5. Midianites (Judges 8:26)
6. Peter (Acts 12:6-7)
7. Nebuchadnezzar (Jeremiah 39:7)
8. Tamar (Genesis 38:28)
9. Pharaoh (Genesis 41:42)
10. Samson (Judges 16:6-9)
11. Jeremiah (40:1)

12. What figure in the New Testament is bound up for a thousand years by a chain?
13. Who arrived in Rome bound by a chain?
14. Who wore an ephod with gold chains on it?
15. Whose servants put ropes on their heads and begged Ahab for mercy?
16. What apostle was on a ship where the ropes holding the lifeboat were deliberately cut?

✦Things on Wheels

1. What prophet's exit is associated with chariots of fire?
2. Who sent back the ark of the covenant on a cart pulled by a cow?
3. What king had 1400 chariots and 12,000 horses?
4. What foreign official was in his chariot when Philip came to him?
5. Who had a vision of four chariots driven by angels?
6. What king burned the idolatrous chariots of the sun?
7. Who took off in his chariot when his tax collector was stoned by the people?
8. Who got to ride in Pharaoh's second chariot?
9. What tribe was given six covered wagons in which to haul the tabernacle and its furnishings?
10. What mighty nation had its chariots ruined in the Red Sea?
11. What king rode into battle in a chariot but was fatally wounded by an Assyrian arrow?
12. Who sent wagons to Canaan to carry back his father and his in-laws?
13. What Syrian leper rode up to Elijah's house in a chariot?
14. What king of Israel was noted as a fast and furious chariot driver?

12. Satan (Revelation 20:1-2)
13. Paul (Acts 28:20)
14. Aaron (Exodus 28:14)
15. The servants of Ben-Hadad (1 Kings 20:31)
16. Paul (Acts 27:30-32)

◆Things on Wheels (Answers)

1. Elijah (2 Kings 2:11)
2. The Philistines (1 Samuel 6:7-14)
3. Solomon (1 Kings 10:26)
4. The Ethiopian eunuch (Acts 8:27-28)
5. Zechariah (6:1-8)
6. Josiah (2 Kings 23:11)
7. Rehoboam (1 Kings 12:18)
8. Joseph (Genesis 41:41, 43)
9. The Levites (Numbers 7:1-9)
10. Egypt (Exodus 14:26-28)
11. Ahab (1 Kings 22:34-38)
12. Joseph (Genesis 45:17-21)
13. Naaman (2 Kings 5:9)
14. Jehu (2 Kings 9:20)

15. What king, fatally wounded while fighting the Egyptians, was brought back to Jerusalem in a chariot?

16. Who had a servant that saw a hillside covered with chariots of fire?

◆The Bible on Screen

1. What controversial 1985 movie starred actor Richard Gere as a king of Israel?

2. Cecil B. DeMille's *The Ten Commandments* (1956), which starred Charlton Heston as Moses, was a remake of a 1923 silent film of the same title. What famous director made the earlier film?

3. What 1966 epic featured director John Huston both as Noah and the voice of God?

4. What much-loved TV movie was directed by Franco Zefferelli, an Italian best known for his work with Shakespeare and opera?

5. In the 1949 film *Samson and Delilah*, directed by Cecil B. DeMille, who played the leading roles?

6. The popular 1943 film *Song of Bernadette* featured actress Linda Darnell in the role of a biblical character. Who did she play?

7. What bald actor, famous for his role in another biblical film, played Solomon (with hair!) in the 1959 film *Solomon and Sheba*?

8. Italian Communist director Pier Paolo Pasolini shocked the world with his 1964 film based on the life of Christ. What was the film's title?

9. What 1981 TV movie starred Anthony Hopkins and Robert Foxworth as two apostles?

10. What 1953 film starred Charles Laughton as a lecherous Herod and Rita Hayworth as the title character?

15. Josiah (2 Chronicles 35:23-24)
16. Elisha (2 Kings 6:14-17)

✦The Bible on Screen (Answers)

1. *King David*
2. Cecil B. DeMille
3. *The Bible*
4. *Jesus of Nazareth*
5. Victor Mature and Hedy Lamarr
6. The Virgin Mary
7. Yul Brynner
8. *The Gospel According to St. Matthew*
9. *Peter and Paul*
10. *Salome*

11. What heartwarming 1963 film with Sidney Poitier took its title from Jesus' statement about "Solomon in all his glory"?

12. What 1932 film showed the declining Roman empire and the growth of the church, and featured Charles Laughton as the despised Emperor Nero?

13. What popular 1953 film, based on a novel by Lloyd Douglas, told the story of Peter and featured such actors as Richard Burton, Jean Simmons, and Victor Mature?

14. This gaudy 1951 film was based on a popular novel by Polish author Henryk Sienkiewicz. It told the story of the early Christians and their persecution under Nero, played by Peter Ustinov. What was the film?

15. This MGM film, made in 1961, was criticized as being "too reverent" in its portrayal of Jesus, played by Jeffrey Hunter. What was the title?

16. Based on a popular stage play, this off-beat 1936 film showed Southern blacks acting out the roles of Old Testament characters. What was the film?

17. In the immensely popular *The Greatest Story Ever Told* (1965), practically every star in Hollywood had a small role. What role, with only one line of dialogue, did John Wayne play in this movie about Jesus?

18. *Ben-Hur*, made in 1959, won 11 of the 12 Academy Awards it was nominated for. What biblical character appeared in the film but did not speak?

19. What 1973 movie, filmed on location in Israel, featured young actors in a musical based on a popular (and controversial) play?

20. Two films—*The Omen* (1976) and *Damien* (1978)—were loosely based on biblical predictions about the Antichrist. What was the title of the third film in the trilogy, in which Christ actually confronts Satan in the final battle?

21. Who played the leading roles in *David and Bathsheba* (1951)?

11. *Lilies of the Field*
12. *The Sign of the Cross*
13. *The Robe*
14. *Quo Vadis?*
15. *King of Kings*
16. *The Green Pastures*
17. The centurion at Jesus' crucifixion (who said, "Truly, this was the son of God")
18. Jesus
19. *Jesus Christ Superstar*
20. *The Final Conflict* (1981)
21. Gregory Peck and Susan Hayward

22. What 1973 musical, based on a stage play taken from the Gospel of Matthew and using old hymns set to new music, was filmed in locations across Manhattan?

23. Comedy director Frank Capra stated that he wanted to cast a popular singer-actor as the lead in his proposed film about the life of Paul. What unlikely star did Capra want?

24. What Paul Newman film about the establishment of the State of Israel has the title of a book of the Bible?

25. What blond Swedish actor played the role of Jesus in *The Greatest Story Ever Told*?

26. What characters from the early years of Jesus' life appear as characters in the film *Ben-Hur*?

27. In the 1956 film *Moby Dick*, which two of the main characters have biblical names?

28. The 1941 film *The Little Foxes*, about a bickering Southern family, takes its title from the Bible. What book of the Bible?

29. What actor, familiar to audiences for his portrayals of gangsters, played the quarrelsome Dathan in *The Ten Comandments*?

30. What 1957 film, based on an Ernest Hemingway novel, took its title from the Book of Ecclesiastes?

31. What extremely controversial 1988 film on the life of Christ earned its director an Academy Award nomination?

32. What violent 1980 film about professional boxing ended with this biblical quote on the screen: "I once was blind, but now I see"?

22. *Godspell*
23. Frank Sinatra
24. *Exodus*
25. Max von Sydow
26. The three wise men
27. Ahab and Ishmael
28. The Song of Solomon 2:15 ("The little foxes that spoil the vines")
29. Edward G. Robinson
30. *The Sun Also Rises*
31. *The Last Temptation of Christ,* directed by Martin Scorsese. The film, incidentally, was not really based on the Bible but on a novel by Greek author Nikos Kazantzakis.
32. *Raging Bull*

✦Not to Be Taken Seriously (II)

1. How do we know there was deviled ham in Bible times? *Math 8:28-32*
2. Where in the Bible does it say people had a Honda auto? *Acts 1:14*
3. Why didn't the last dove return to the ark?
4. What city was named after something you find on a car? *Josh 19:29*
5. Why was the kangaroo the most miserable animal on the ark?
6. Where did the Israelites keep their money?
7. What time was it when the elephant sat on Noah's chair?
8. What vegetable did Noah refuse to take on the ark?
9. Why was the Red Sea angry? *Ex 14:22, 29*
10. What was the rudest animal on the ark?
11. What did the skunks have that no other animals on the ark have?
12. What is the sleepiest land in the Bible? *Gen 4:16,17*
13. Where were freeways first mentioned in the Bible? *Gen 1:30*
14. Why did the tower of Babel stand in the land of Shinar? *Gen 11:1-9*
15. What was in the wall of Jerusalem that the Israelites did not put there?
16. How many species of animals did Noah take into the ark?
17. Was there money on Noah's ark?

✦Not to Be Taken Seriously (II) (Answers)

1. Devils went into a herd of swine.
2. Acts 1:14—"They all continued with one accord."
3. She had found sufficient grounds to stay away.
4. Tyre
5. Her children had to play inside on rainy days.
6. The banks of the Jordan
7. Time to get a new chair
8. Leeks
9. The children of Israel crossed it.
10. The mockingbird
11. Baby skunks
12. The land of Nod
13. Genesis 1:30—"The Lord made every creeping thing."
14. It would have looked funny lying on its side.
15. Cracks
16. All of them
17. Yes—the duck had a bill, the skunk had a scent, and the frog had a greenback.

Other Living Books Best-sellers

THE ANGEL OF HIS PRESENCE by Grace Livingston Hill. This book captures the romance of John Wentworth Stanley and a beautiful young woman whose influence causes John to re-evaluate his well-laid plans for the future. 07-0047 $3.95.

ANSWERS by Josh McDowell and Don Stewart. In a question-and-answer format, the authors tackle sixty-five of the most-asked questions about the Bible, God, Jesus Christ, miracles, other religions, and creation. 07-0021 $4.95.

THE BEST CHRISTMAS PAGEANT EVER by Barbara Robinson. A delightfully wild and funny story about what happens to a Christmas program when the "Horrible Herdman" brothers and sisters are miscast in the roles of the biblical Christmas story characters. 07-0137 $3.95.

BUILDING YOUR SELF IMAGE by Josh McDowell. Here are practical answers to help you overcome your fears, anxieties, and lack of self-confidence. Learn how God's higher image of who you are can take root in your heart and mind. 07-1395 $4.50.

THE CHILD WITHIN by Mari Hanes. The author shares insights she gained from God's Word during her own pregnancy. She identifies areas of stress, offers concrete data about the birth process, and points to God's sure promises that he will "gently lead those that are with young." 07-0219 $3.95.

COME BEFORE WINTER AND SHARE MY HOPE by Charles R. Swindoll. A collection of brief vignettes offering hope and the assurance that adversity and despair are temporary setbacks we can overcome! 07-0477 $6.95.

DARE TO DISCIPLINE by James Dobson. A straightforward, plainly written discussion about building and maintaining parent/child relationships based upon love, respect, authority, and ultimate loyalty to God. 07-0522 $4.95.

DAVID AND BATHSHEBA by Roberta Kells Dorr. This novel combines solid biblical and historical research with suspenseful storytelling about men and women locked in the eternal struggle for power, governed by appetites they wrestle to control. 07-0618 $4.95.

Other Living Books Best-sellers

DR. DOBSON ANSWERS YOUR QUESTIONS by James Dobson. In this convenient reference book, renowned author Dr. James Dobson addresses heartfelt concerns on many topics including marital relationships, infant care, child discipline, home management, and others. 07-0580 $4.95.

FOR MEN ONLY edited by J. Allan Petersen. This book deals with topics of concern to every man: the business world, marriage, fathering, spiritual goals, and problems of living as a Christian in a secular world. 07-0892 $4.95.

FOR WOMEN ONLY by Evelyn and J. Allan Petersen. Balanced, entertaining, diversified treatment of all aspects of womanhood. 07-0897 $5.95.

400 WAYS TO SAY I LOVE YOU by Alice Chapin. Perhaps the flame of love has almost died in your marriage. Maybe you have a good marriage that just needs a little "spark." Here is a book especially for the woman who wants to rekindle the flame of romance in her marriage. With creative, practical ideas on how to show the man in her life that she cares. 07-0919 $3.95.

GIVERS, TAKERS, AND OTHER KINDS OF LOVERS by Josh McDowell and Paul Lewis. This book bypasses vague generalities about love and sex and gets right to the basic questions: Whatever happened to sexual freedom? What's true love like? Do men respond differently than women? If you're looking for straight answers about God's plan for love and sexuality, this book was written for you. 07-1031 $3.95.

HINDS' FEET ON HIGH PLACES by Hannah Hurnard. A classic allegory of a journey toward faith that has sold more than a million copies! 07-1429 $4.95.

HOW TO BE HAPPY THOUGH MARRIED by Tim LaHaye. One of America's most successful marriage counselors gives practical, proven advice for marital happiness. 07-1499 $3.95.

JOHN, SON OF THUNDER by Ellen Gunderson Traylor. In this saga of adventure, travel with John — the disciple whom Jesus loved — down desert paths, through the courts of the Holy City, to the foot of the cross, leaving his luxury as a privileged son of Israel for the bitter hardship of his exile on Patmos. 07-1903 $5.95.

Other Living Books Best-sellers

LIFE IS TREMENDOUS! by Charlie "Tremendous" Jones. Believing that enthusiasm makes the difference, Jones shows how anyone can be happy, involved, relevant, productive, healthy, and secure in the midst of a high-pressure, commercialized society. 07-2184 $3.50.

LORD, COULD YOU HURRY A LITTLE? by Ruth Harms Calkin. These prayer-poems from the heart of a godly woman trace the inner workings of the heart, following the rhythms of the day and seasons of the year with expectation and love. 07-3816 $3.50.

LORD, I KEEP RUNNING BACK TO YOU by Ruth Harms Calkin. In prayer-poems tinged with wonder, joy, humanness, and questioning, the author speaks for all of us who are groping and learning together what it means to be God's child. 07-3819 $3.95.

MORE THAN A CARPENTER by Josh McDowell. A hard-hitting book for people who are skeptical about Jesus' deity, his resurrection, and his claim on their lives. 07-4552 $3.95.

MOUNTAINS OF SPICES by Hannah Hurnard. Here is an allegory comparing the nine spices mentioned in the Song of Solomon to the nine fruits of the Spirit. A story of the glory of surrender by the author of **Hinds' Feet on High Places**. 07-4611 $4.50.

NOW IS YOUR TIME TO WIN by Dave Dean. In this true-life story, Dean shares how he locked into seven principles that enabled him to bounce back from failure to success. Read about successful men and women — from sports and entertainment celebrities to the ordinary people next door — and discover how you too can bounce back from failure to success! 07-4727 $3.95.

THE SECRET OF LOVING by Josh McDowell. McDowell explores the values and qualities that will help both the single and married reader to be the right person for someone else. He offers a fresh perspective for evaluating and improving the reader's love life. 07-5845 $4.95.

THE STORY FROM THE BOOK. The full sweep of **The Book**'s contents in abridged, chronological form, giving the reader the "big picture" of the Bible. 07-6677 $4.95.

Other Living Books Best-sellers

STRIKE THE ORIGINAL MATCH by Charles Swindoll. Many couples ask: What do you do when the warm, passionate fire that once lit your marriage begins to wane? Here, Chuck Swindoll provides biblical steps for rekindling the fires of romance and building marital intimacy. 07-6445-5 $4.95.

SUCCESS: THE GLENN BLAND METHOD by Glenn Bland. The author shows how to set goals and make plans that really work. His ingredients for success include spiritual, financial, educational, and recreational balances. 07-6689 $4.95.

THROUGH GATES OF SPLENDOR by Elisabeth Elliott. This unforgettable story of five men who braved the Auca Indians has become one of the most famous missionary books of all times. 07-7151 $4.95.

WHAT WIVES WISH THEIR HUSBANDS KNEW ABOUT WOMEN by James Dobson. The best-selling author of **Dare to Discipline** and **The Strong-Willed Child** brings us this vital book that speaks to the unique emotional needs and aspirations of today's woman. An immensely practical, interesting guide. 07-7896 $3.95.

WHY YOU ACT THE WAY YOU DO by Tim LaHaye. Discover how your temperament affects your work, emotions, spiritual life, and relationships and learn how to make improvements. 07-8212 $4.95.

You can find all of these Living Books at your local Christian bookstore. If they are unavailable, send check or money order for retail price plus $1.00 postage and handling per book (U.S. and territories only) to:

Tyndale D.M.S., Box 80, Wheaton, IL 60189

Prices and availability subject to change without notice.

Please allow 4-6 weeks for delivery.